Disaster Plan

A Memoir

Eric Tallman

This is a true story. The characters in this book are all based on real people. For the sake of privacy I have changed all real names to fictional versions. Some events have been modified.

Chapter 1

I am a member of an international society of experts. So is my neighbor with the tattoo of a hundred dollar bill etched into his left bicep, and the checkout clerk who works at the local grocery store, and the woman in electric blue shorts who jogs past my house two mornings a week. We do not discriminate. People of every gender, race, religion, ethnicity, sexual orientation and age are welcome. Conservatives and liberals are welcome. Christians, Jews and Muslims are welcome. Socialists, capitalists, gays, straights, atheists, soccer moms, NASCAR dads, welcome, welcome, welcome.

Our club has never gathered for long weekends of communal revelry, a beloved ritual for most groups. Our differences in cultures, practices and beliefs are too stark to risk these kinds of gatherings. Social interaction among our members could result in dangerously unsocial acts. The majority of us will remain strangers forever, oblivious to the slender philosophical thread that connects our lives.

Qualification for enrollment is easy. Any individual can join. Membership may lack official credentials or the stamp of an accredited institution but it comes with an impressive new job title: *disaster expert*. We embrace our new role eagerly. We are committed to thwarting the violent acts of nature that strike the communities where we live. Our participation is driven by a fear of unchecked catastrophe but also by a more inspired motivation: we view disaster preparation as a creative challenge. The evacuation routes that we map with rulers and colored pencils, the shelves and cabinets that we skillfully bolt to the walls of our houses, the bins that we fill with meticulous layers of life-saving supplies are our works of artistic genius.

Our levels of proficiency range from the enthusiastic amateur proudly displaying a cardboard box lovingly packed with canned soup and bottled water to the consummate survivalist posed in front of the entrance to his underground bunker wearing full camo gear and draped in weaponry. Most of us fall somewhere in the middle of these two extremes, the moderate club members who haven't created an exhaustive color-coded spreadsheet of every stored item nor those devotees whose kit consists of a bottle of premium tequila accompanied by a vow to ride out the big one like a surfer crouched in the barrel of a wave.

Disaster experts inhabit every corner of our planet, but the geographical regions where cataclysms strike with fearsome regularity contain the highest concentration of club members.

California is one of these locations. Even though this celebrated piece of United States geography, dangling at the edge of the Pacific Ocean, is subject to some of the most violent natural phenomenon on this planet, tens of millions of people have chosen these coastlines, mountains, deserts and valleys as their permanent home. We thrive among the blend of beauty and danger that is molded into one breathtaking dramatic package.

Those of us who grew up here are on intimate terms with the earthquakes that rock our state from its far northern coastline to its southern border. In our first classroom, where dozens of kindergartners discover the salty taste of Play-Doh, the catharsis of finger painting and the power of the temper tantrum as a negotiating tool in difficult toy transactions, we receive our first exposure to the destructive power of earthquakes.

We scramble under the arts and crafts tables during our first duck-and-cover drill, excitedly participating in this new game before returning to our play group when released from our position by our teacher.

We will practice this safety exercise annually during our twelve year progression through the educational system. The physical act of crawling under a desk or table will remain unchanged but new material will catalyze the curriculum. The teacher will give a reading assignment that will include survivors' stories of living through the 1906 San Francisco earthquake or we will be given homework to draw a diagram of the geological plates that grasp each other in a tectonic headlock beneath the ocean floor. These classrooms of our elementary, middle school and high school years are forums for the objective study of earthquakes, but they are also laboratories for real-time exposure to the fickle power of the earth.

Earthquakes can arrive with an explosive blast of energy or they can make a more prolonged entrance, announcing their arrival with a low rumble that builds into a thundering dramatic performance. Posts and beams will groan as they shift within their seismic fittings. Window blinds along the classroom walls will rattle like skeletons in a haunted house, chalk will skitter in its metal trough, the pencils in front of us will assume an eerie sentience, rolling back and forth across the desk. During the first few seconds we glance around the room, assessing the level of danger. Then we initiate our emergency routine, dropping to the floor, knees pressed against the linoleum, heads ducked and shielded by our arms and hands. The shaking will most likely end almost as quickly as it began. We will revel for a moment in the sudden silence, a stillness disrupted only by the rustle of hunched bodies extricating themselves from their cramped positions before students seize the opportunity to burst into raucous conversation. The excitement will subside only when the adrenaline finally does.

Hundreds of minor seismic events occur each week in California. The vast majority of these temblors are undetectable to humans. We drive, walk, eat and sleep through constant minute shifts in the earth's crust that are recognized only by the the network of scientific equipment implanted throughout the state.

The deadly earthquakes that deliver waves of destruction to everything in their path receive much greater attention. Their devastation directly impacts thousands or millions of people who live within range of the shock waves but their notoriety explodes even further outward within minutes of the event, saturating every corner of the planet with sensational videos and photos that feed the insatiable appetite of an international audience.

I experienced the 1989 Loma Prieta earthquake in my second floor apartment in San Francisco, standing in the middle of the living room while my cat performed heroic gymnastics at my feet, trying to keep himself physically removed from the rolling, heaving floor. Each time his paws hit the carpet he would spring straight up into the air again. After several bouts of these jarring movements he realized the window was open and leapt through it. I watched him disappear across the roof next door, frantically racing away. He would return hours later, skulking towards his food bowl, ready to flee again at the slightest indication of movement.

My living room was an interior designer's nightmare of insufferable neglect. It was a small, bare space devoid of décor or artwork and occupied by a thrift store sofa pushed against a wall. My roommate and I treated this room as a transit corridor, a place to pass through on the way to work, sleep, bars, dates or the houses of friends.

I stood in the center of the room and shifted my weight to counter the motion of the rippling floor. Any panicky urge to seek shelter beneath the kitchen table was alleviated by the spartan setting.

My most pervasive memory of the event was the noise. The deep rumbling of the earth provided a sustained counterpoint to a high-pitched percussive clatter. Every item in the apartment that wasn't solidly moored jumped and shook in a jittery frenzy. Dishes in their cupboards, the silverware in the drawers, the glasses and cups in the sink, the pencils, change, keys, jewelry and trinkets on tables and counters all clattered fiercely. The walls creaked as they strained against the forces trying to contort them. The entire building was playing a composition written for an orchestra of kinetic architecture.

Fifteen seconds after the violent shuddering started, it stopped. Like a surreal power failure, someone had flipped the switch that controlled all motion and sound for an apartment building, a city block and a sprawling metropolis. I stood at the center of this silent universe, listening to the rapid intake and exhalation of my breath.

I hurried down the hall to the back door, stepping over a roll of toilet paper that had bounced out of the bathroom and unraveled in a long strand. In the kitchen I saw pieces of shattered plates on the floor and a coffee carafe that teetered at the stove's edge. I pulled the back door open and gingerly tested the deck with the toe of my shoe before stepping on to it.

Two words raced through my mind, forming a mantra: gas and water, gas and water, gas and water. They had been embedded in my conscience by a lifetime of earthquake awareness.

The back porch glistened with a fine layer of water that dampened trash cans and potted plants. A spray hissed from a cracked connection that led to the water heater. I grabbed the handle to the metal valve and twisted it shut.

I entered the apartment again, sniffing like a human bloodhound, my nose thrust in the air. Only the familiar odor of musty brown carpet invaded my nostrils. No gas was leaking, no walls had fractured into a web of cracks, no floors had buckled, no ceilings had crumbled.

My next destination had the potential for an even more vivid landscape of violence and destruction. I paused for a moment before pulling the front door open and descending the flight of exterior stairs.

The street that I lived on during that five year period of my life was an anomaly within the heart of San Francisco. Traffic roared through the center of the city all day and evening, a grind of brakes and blare of acceleration that was a ceaseless soundtrack for the residents who lived in the apartment buildings that flanked these wide thoroughfares. The short street where my apartment was located terminated in a dead end. A large storage lot for the public works department, encased in chain link fence, was an imposing barrier that discouraged entrance into our block-long street. Only a few cars and trucks intruded on our small piece of South of Market real estate.

We were a natural destination for the traumatized residents and employees of the nearby residential buildings, restaurants, auto shops, small warehouses and retail stores seeking the safety of open space. I stepped from the sidewalk and into the street, joining the growing crowd.

The earthquake had sent its waves across the city shortly after 5:00 PM. We were approaching the twilight hour. The asphalt and sidewalk were scattered with lengthening shadows.

A man with a bandana tied across his forehead and bushy sideburns that crept far below his jawline cradled a radio in his hands, our own grizzled prophet bringing tidings of disaster to our neighborhood. We huddled in a half-circle, staring at this small battery-powered device like it was a miracle of modern communication. In 1989 mobile phones were still the extravagant tool and toy of technophiles and business executives. For the next several days our cheap radios, dug out of closets and drawers and brought to public venues, would be our lifeline to the world.

The local radio news channels were locked in a competition to capture the attention of an audience living in a state of shock. As we mingled in the street on that unusually warm October evening we heard that the Bay Bridge had collapsed, then that it hadn't, then that it had. We were informed that hundreds were feared dead, then that casualties were limited because the World Series game in nearby Candlestick Park that pitted local baseball teams the Oakland Athletics against the San Francisco Giants in a contentious rivalry had reduced rush hour traffic to an extraordinary low. Breathless updates were the norm. Accurate information would come later. We knew that fires burned, not too far away, because we could smell smoke.

Periodically I would look east and watch the intersection where my narrow street met the imposing width and congestion of Fourth Street. I had learned, from years of driving down that busy thoroughfare, the strategy for avoiding the right lane that narrowed into a congested funnel of vehicles as drivers made the slow crawl towards the nearby Interstate 280 on-ramp.

Now Fourth St. was a parking lot. Cars were stopped in the middle of intersections ruled by anarchy instead of stoplights, trying to reach freeways that were just as impassable. My roommate Phillip would soon emerge from this standstill of idling cars, trucks and buses, gliding on to our street on the motorcycle that allowed him to roll home through immobilized columns of traffic.

The twilight on the horizon was hazy red, the wail of sirens was an apocalyptic symphony and the flashlights that neighbors flickered in the fading light cast piercing beams across the outdoor setting. I felt an unnerving sense of being a character in a dramatic performance, written by an omniscient playwright testing the emotions and stamina of a group of strangers thrust together under duress.

Phillip and I quickly learned the art of urban camping. We sorted through the assortment of canned foods in our kitchen cupboard. Our meals defied every modicum of decency. Garbanzo beans, tuna fish and tortilla chips stirred into a bowl produced food that was a beige mass and had the consistency of damp mortar. We ended our first dining experience with a quart of chocolate chip ice cream, knowing its doomed future in a freezer that would soon be an incubator for seething bacteria. Corn flakes mixed with a can of sliced peaches made a sweet and syrupy breakfast. We sipped from several unopened plastic bottles of water in the refrigerator. We placed half a dozen candles around the apartment, igniting them each evening like characters in a modern gothic novel. No ambient illumination from streetlights or storefronts penetrated the darkness that obscured the corners of the rooms. The electrical grid had failed throughout the majority of San Francisco. Our neighborhood was as black as any haunted British moor on a moonless night.

Fortunately our landlord prioritized the repair of the leaking pipes and restored running water within twenty four hours. The electricity and gas remained off, the streets of our neighborhood were dangerous to navigate and the front doors to our local corner market were locked. We were lucky. Two blocks away from the street where we gathered daily in front of my apartment building the exterior brick wall of a four story building had cascaded to the street below in a mass of lethal rubble, killing five people in seconds. A long double-decker section of freeway in Oakland had collapsed, killing dozens of drivers in their cars. Fires burned through multiple buildings in the Marina District. Our three-day aftermath left us spooning chunks of tepid food into our mouths and shivering through cold showers. In our private moments we were grateful for every moment of inconvenience. Nature had exempted us from her wrath not out of preference but simply from oversight. We knew she would return again in an even greater rage in the near or distant future.

I created my first disaster kit within a month of the Loma Prieta earthquake while the urgency of the event still lingered. A flashlight, radio, batteries, a jug of water, an assortment of canned and freeze-dried foods, candles, matches and a first aid kit were the supplies that I stacked into a cardboard box. It was a concentrated version of the items that Phillip and I had hurriedly scrounged from the corners of our apartment in the hours that followed the earthquake. I didn't know then that the simple container that I placed on the floor of my bedroom closet was a first step towards mastering a new form of craftsmanship. I was honing my creative vision. My finest work was still to come.

Chapter 2

Earthquakes destroy but they also unite. Buildings topple, streets buckle, technology fails, continental plates are plied apart. The rending of inanimate objects is brute and unforgiving.

These geological upheavals have the opposite effect on the bond between the people who survive them. As soon as the shaking stops, as soon as we perform a hurried self-examination to confirm that no blood seeps from any wound and that our nearby fellow humans are uninjured, we seek companionship. I was never alone during the hours I spent in front of my house in the aftermath of the destruction, sitting on my front steps or loitering on the sidewalk. I met neighbors I had passed on my street for years without exchanging more than a brief hello. Now we engaged in extended conversations. Natural gas explosions, contaminated drinking water, rat swarms and the tenuous line between life and death were some of the weighty subjects that we discussed in detail.

The importance of human interaction lasts long after emergency recovery efforts have subsided. The invisible urban armor that normally protects us is more malleable as we exchange greetings with people we would normally keep at the periphery of our vision in grocery stores, subways and other public places.

Almost a year after the fires had been extinguished, the collapsed buildings cordoned and the damaged freeways closed the daily routine of most Bay Area residents had returned to normal. One Saturday evening I took the bus to a party at the apartment of several friends. I engaged in my usual analysis of the gallery of faces, hairstyles, outfits and mutterings of my fellow riders as the bus lurched towards my destination.

We gathered my friends' flat in the Castro district of San Francisco. Martinis were our chosen drink that evening, a cocktail that had the ring of sophistication favored by accomplished drinkers in their early thirties. The hosts had complemented the drinks with a platter of appetizers, a spread that served as both a social hub for the party and a practical method for mediating the effects of hard liquor on empty stomachs.

I was in the living room, sitting cross-legged on the hardwood floor. A small bag of marijuana and a packet of cigarette papers were balanced in my lap. The joint that I was rolling wasn't intended for personal use but served a more selfless purpose. Several of my friends were sitting on a nearby couch, sprawled across the cushions in such an intertwined fashion that they looked like a six-legged, three-headed human beast. This creature had expressed, in a blend of overlapping voices, a desire to get high. I had offered my services as an act of benevolence.

I pursued my task with the concentration of a musician immersed in a complex solo, finessing the crumbled bud into the rolling paper, trying not to accidentally dump the contents onto the floor. My friends on the couch giggled as I hunched forward and concentrated on my work. With a quick motion I licked the length of the gummed edge and nimbly twisted the seam closed.

The finished joint looked like a miniature version of a caveman's hunting club. It had a dent in the middle and a hump at its tip. I cupped it in my hand while I prepared myself for the humiliation of public exposure. Then I raised it into view.

The response from the couch was swift. An

arm unfolded from the collection of body parts, plucked the joint from my hand, and put it into smoldering circulation. The beast's need to get high clearly overrode any urge to mock my competence.

With my job complete and embarrassment averted, I turned my attention back to the room around me.

Another guest was seated near me in a similar cross-legged position, his attention directed towards two people sitting next to him on a pair of low red vinyl chairs. Each member of this talkative group leaned inward to form an intimate trio. Periodically a burst of laughter would peak above the music that blasted from stereo speakers in the corners of the room.

I was surprised when my neighbor turned away from his companions and smiled at me. My reaction was reflexive. I smiled in return, felt a flush of self-consciousness, and turned away to carefully examine a large painting hanging above the fireplace. Even though I'd spent hours in the presence of this artwork during the many times I'd visited this apartment, I had barely glanced at it. Now I methodically counted the number of abstract shapes that filled the canvas. When I reached a total of twenty I turned my attention back to the other occupant of this patch of living room floor.

He mouthed the word hello to me. I cupped my hand to my ear and slid across the smooth surface until I was facing him.

We quickly embarked down the meandering path of party talk. Anecdotes about jobs, travel, gruesome diseases and albino mammals are just some of the topics that break the ice between two strangers at a social gathering. The volume of our voices rose and fell in response to the decibel level of each song that played. Periodically our conversation would lapse into awkward silence and then resume its momentum, sustained by the strong undercurrent of two young men energized by a boisterous party and an unmistakable attraction to each other.

My new friend and I quickly landed on the theme that dominated conversations throughout the Bay Area that year. I told him my earthquake story and he told me his.

Daniel performed a comic reenactment of his flailing hands on the steering wheel of his car when the earthquake struck. The vehicle suddenly defied his attempts to follow the contours of the road. His two passengers chided him, demanding that he drive more carefully. This nagging choir quickly fell silent when they all realized they were experiencing a major earthquake. Daniel wound his way back to his apartment using side streets that only a long-term resident of San Francisco would know. He dropped his friends along the way so they could join the flow of pedestrians

I took a sip of my drink and I told him about my cat and its attempts to become the first feline in space. Our voices grew more animated as we drained our drinks.

Our initial encounter eventually ended but we both knew the relationship had just begun. Our similarities were too compelling to ignore. We were creatively driven, we acquired much of our wardrobes and furniture from thrift stores, we were oblivious to bad hair days, we were irreverent, we were cynical. I was thrilled that I had finally met someone who was as weird as me.

Romantic infatuation in its earliest phase outranks perfectly chilled Martinis and pungent marijuana. The intoxication isn't restricted to the physical proximity of the new object of our affection. It influences every aspect of our lives. Suddenly I was passionate about shopping for dish soap and toothpaste. I was perplexed to find myself sympathizing with the customers in the restaurant where I worked as they pestered me for water refills, clean silverware, extra napkins. The drive in my car to Daniel's apartment was a blissful journey devoid of the irritating effects of potholes, blaring horns and maddeningly slow drivers. Daniel and I had found each other. This was the relationship that we had both been waiting for and the partner we both wanted it with.

We veered into the dating fast lane. The days spent in each other's company started to outnumber the days spent apart. My toothbrush joined his in the water glass on the counter of his bathroom. My own apartment became a place to gather clothes, pick up my mail and exchange greetings with Phillip before returning to my second home.

The decision to live together was easy. We had reached the level of familiarity with each other where we spoke in the first-person plural with annoying regularity: we are planning a trip, we invite you to our house, we love your new haircut, we are cooking spaghetti alfredo tonight. We finally celebrated the gay version of marriage in the 1990s, long before same-sex marriage became legal in California or the United States, when we adopted our first dog together.

One summer morning Daniel and I woke in our bed in our apartment in San Francisco, pushed the down comforter aside, placed our bare feet on the chilly floor, pulled on our typical morning outfits of jeans, sweaters, socks and knit hats, turned the wall heater to high, watched the steam from our coffee cups evaporate into the brisk kitchen air and called a real estate agent. We explained to her that we'd heard stories of nearby cities so warm and devoid of dripping August fog and blasting wind that a person could wear a t-shirt outside without risking hypothermia. There were rumors of properties with yards big enough to hold a picnic table with benches and still leave room for a lawn deer. The prices on many houses were rumored to be in a range that people who weren't vested millionaires or trust fund recipients could afford.

Daniel and I spent hours in the aging Mercedes that our agent steered through the streets of the East Bay. This was our first foray into the process of buying a house and we were invigorated. We knew that this adventure would culminate in a spacious new home surrounded by a small but verdant yard.

We struggled to maintain our buoyant attitude through successive journeys that began to feel like persecution rather than pleasure. Our modest budget put a starkly realistic limit on our options.

The string of dwellings we visited suffered from varying levels of dilapidation. Crumbling foundations, cracked drywall, crack houses and massive repair bills were the lurking pitfalls that ambushed optimistic buyers.

Almost two weeks into this odyssey our agent told us she had a listing in Oakland that was unusual and unique. I scowled in the back seat, alert to these code words for another piece of real estate sinking into decay. The frustration that Daniel and I felt was wearing our patience to a dangerously thin veneer.

The initial view of the house revealed a narrow two story Victorian built in the early 1900s. I allowed a glimmer of leniency into my cynical outlook when I saw that the exterior paint wasn't peeling away from the window frames and that the front stairs were devoid of rotting wood eager to consume an ascending or descending foot.

A tour of the interior revealed three small bedrooms and a cramped bathroom upstairs, a traditional layout for Victorians from that era. Our agent led us through a small living room and parlor downstairs that had undoubtedly served as the social hub for card games and sherry sipped from stemmed glasses on Saturday nights a hundred years earlier.

Daniel and I passed through the final doorway on the tour and we both gasped in astonishment. We had entered a vast kitchen. It had been built as an addition to the house in the 1970s and contained enough counter space to operate an industrial-sized restaurant. Rows of cherry wood cabinets ran along the upper and lower parameters of three walls. The room seemed as large as an entire studio apartment in San Francisco. I immediately envisioned a massive farmhouse style table surrounded by eight chairs in the center of this large space.

Daniel and I wandered from one end of the kitchen to the other, peering into the cupboards and imagining savory meals simmering in pots on the residential Wolf range.

The next shock of disbelief came when we stepped out the back door. The backyard sprawled to a far wooden fence. A massive oak tree in the middle of this expanse had the coarse bark and thick limbs that revealed a century of gnarled grace.

Our agent was right. The house was quirky and odd. The giant modern kitchen clashed with the Victorian character of the original structure. The building was probably haunted by the restless ghosts of past inhabitants. After one day of deliberation Daniel and I made an offer. Our agent nodded sagely as she slid the first stack of paperwork in front of us.

Three months later we moved into our new home. We proclaimed our love for the cozy bedrooms. We wandered dreamily through the kitchen. Our bulky jackets drifted, ignored, to the back of our closets. A picnic table and newly planted shrubs fit perfectly next to a row of white picket fence we installed. Our commute time to work in San Francisco doubled but the square footage of our living space had nearly tripled.

We felt like pioneers striking out into uncharted territory. Cell phones were crude devices in that era, not yet capable of guiding perplexed drivers to unknown destinations with crisp confidence. My car was littered with street maps creased into oversized origami. We would depart from our house bickering over the correct route to take to a new location.

Our steady progress towards translating the baffling network of streets and landmarks into recognizable neighborhoods brought a growing sense of accomplishment, but there was an even more profound transition occurring in our lives.

San Francisco can have a hypnotic influence on its residents. This glittering city, draped across jutting hills and juxtaposed against shimmering water, has the power to confound the logic of otherwise rational people. Traveling beyond its borders can cause palpitations in the hardiest of inhabitants. Devoted fans know that the dozens of smaller cities that form a ring around the Bay, sprawling outward to the north, east and south, are privileged to be dwelling in the refracted beauty of the Bay Area's crown jewel.

Before moving to the East Bay Daniel and I had pragmatically accepted our inevitable sacrifice of world class food, art, entertainment and culture for the opportunity to own a house and see the sun shine for days on end. The geographical distance from downtown Oakland to downtown San Francisco is only nine miles driving distance but the psychological distance is vast.

We were startled at the depth of our miscalculation. Instead of landing in a ghost town where restaurants closed their doors by 9:00 PM and nightlife was restricted to a few meager bars and clubs we discovered a hidden treasure. Oakland had not yet experienced the incursion of exorbitantly priced bars and restaurants, skyrocketing real estate prices, pretentious nightclubs, mega-millionaires and eager newcomers looking for the mind-altering experiences that San Francisco notoriously offered. Oakland was grounded in generations of neighborhoods and families that had made the city a fertile ground for some of the best music, art and food in the world, without any of the hyperbole.

We filled our house with furniture and objects, loading the kitchen cupboards and drawers with all the implements necessary for cooking elaborate meals, furnishing every blank space with thrift store treasures. We painted walls and ceilings and we shored the wooden backyard deck. Our new neighbors gradually became our friends. Our casual social gatherings expanded into parties. We realized our dream of sitting outdoors at night with elbows and knees exposed to the warm evening air.

Eventually we took an exponential leap forward. Years after our arrival in the East Bay we sold our first house and bought a new one. The wide backyard with a steep upward slope was the perfect setting for the urban farm that we planned and our roles as the gentlemen farmers that we were eager to assume. Oakland had long ceased to be a mystery. It was home.

One afternoon as I sat at our kitchen table, trying to convince myself that gazing lazily out the back window at our flock of hens scratching through the compacted soil was an acceptable alternative to cleaning the crusty piles of droppings that had reached a disturbing new depth in the chicken coop, I heard the electronic notification on my computer that a new email had just arrived in my inbox. Any distraction was preferred to the guilt of my neglect, so I opened the email.

It was from a friend who lived in San Francisco. The subject line consisted of the three words: "It's your FAULT!!!" I stared with irritation at this onslaught of exclamation marks, then opened the email.

My eyes gravitated to a rectangular map located near the middle of the page. The image showed a satellite view of the East Bay. I recognized the long string of cities that formed a continuous sprawl from Richmond in the north to Hayward in the south. Oakland occupied the biggest chunk of the map, an asymmetrical outline located near the middle of the image.

A bold red vertical line ran the length of the map, its continuity broken at several points into smaller dashed sections. The line slashed through the freeways and major streets that formed the most prominent reference points. I frowned and started reading the text above the image.

A byline for a newspaper was printed at the top of the page. My friend had forwarded an article from a local news site. The first paragraphs summarized an event that had occurred in a past century. In October 1868 a major earthquake had unleashed an explosion of energy along the Hayward fault. This subterranean fissure, marked with such a vivid line on the map, had sent waves of destruction undulating in every direction.

The East Bay in 1868 was an expanse of open hills and flatlands dotted with small cities still subject to the rituals and rhythms of rural life. Dozens of people died in this sparsely populated territory. The event was quickly dubbed The Great San Francisco Earthquake, a title that would define this disaster for almost forty years until a more infamous earthquake would strike in 1906 and claim exclusive rights to the name.

On the lower section of the page another string of exaggerated text demanded my attention. These words had been crowned with a second cluster of exclamation marks. "Now comes the fun part!!!" it said. I vowed to pry the exclamation key off my friend's laptop the next time I visited him at his grubby little apartment in San Francisco.

The next few paragraphs informed me that the Hayward fault delivers an earthquake to the region approximately every 140 years. Soil samples from deep in the earth have revealed an alarming fact. This jagged fault line has been adhering to a strict schedule for centuries. The article concluded its narrative with a summation that surely brought a snicker of glee to my friend. The 140th anniversary had arrived. 2008 was the year that Oakland, and most of the East Bay, was at the top of the guest list for an anniversary party that none of us wanted to attend.

Until this unsolicited information had arrived in my inbox, Daniel and I had naively assumed we were moving away from danger, not toward it. A lifetime of earthquake awareness had focused my attention on one seismological superstar as the prime candidate for the next big earthquake. The San Andreas fault is the mother of all California faults, slashing its way through the state from north to south and cutting through the ocean just west of the Golden Gate. It is as much a part of the history of San Francisco as the little cable cars that climb halfway to the stars, dodging swerving drivers and tipsy tourists, and the hippies that launched a revolution of love and hallucinations in the 1960s. The Hayward fault was a hairline crack in the earth in comparison to this mighty force lying just to the west.

When we bought our second house our real estate agent had mentioned the Hayward fault as if it were a passing annoyance. Daniel and I responded with similar indifference. We signed the disclosure sheets that listed all the improbable catastrophes that could strike. We were joining the ranks of hundreds of thousands of homeowners, employees and commuters who lived, worked or traveled on the Hayward fault. They had survived here for generations and so would we.

Now this toxic seed, planted by my friend, found fertile soil. Daniel and I were part of the vast society of Bay Area residents who had voluntarily drained their savings accounts and gone into years of debt to become homeowners in one of the most booming real estate markets in the nation. If the house collapsed because of our irresponsibility our future could collapse with it. Financial uncertainty had forged us into responsible adults.

We hired a construction crew to install shear wall and bolt the foundations of our house. While they hammered and drilled in the crawl space below the floorboards we attended to our own project above. We opened our aging disaster preparation kit and sorted through the contents. The majority of the contents went into the trash, an unsightly heap of expired foods, corroded batteries and desiccated first aid supplies. Online research guided crucial new choices: a camp stove, fuel canisters, extra clothing, water purification tablets, sunscreen, five jugs of drinking water, $200 in small bills, solar blankets and a bottle of whisky. All found their niche in our upgraded collection of goods.

We invested in two large plastic bins and carefully fit everything into a snug package. This pair of containers received a prime location on an easily accessible shelf in our garage. They were humble and imposing, squat and elegant, and a proud reminder that Daniel and I had advanced to an expert level of preparedness. We were ready for any disaster that might strike.

Chapter 3

It's easy to make plans for the last Sunday in June in San Francisco. Every year tens of thousands of people board flights and map the freeways that lead them to the annual SF Pride celebration. In the 1970s, years before dozens of huge corporations such as Bank of America, AT&T and Walt Disney decided that the profitability of promoting their products to a derided demographic outweighed the risk of public controversy, the event was simply known as the gay parade. This celebration that wound through the streets of San Francisco was a mix of street theatre, anarchic politics and recreational substances. In an era when homosexual acts were still punishable by imprisonment in many states of the U.S.A., we had one day a year to engage in unencumbered displays of public affection and unfamiliar feelings of self-worth.

The parade is now attended by over a million

people. The abbreviation LGBTQ rolls of the tongues of elected officials across the spectrum, from staunchly conservative leaders uttering this string of consonants as if they were laced with venom to liberal politicians pronouncing each letter effortlessly. Gay pride is no longer the exclusive domain of the gays. Straight families stand next to gay families along the crowded parade route, all cheering the same floats full of giddy revelers and festooned convertibles carrying drag queen royalty and local dignitaries.

The main event commences on Sunday morning when the Dykes On Bikes start their engines and launch the official start of the Pride parade. For one day the financial district in downtown San Francisco is devoid of sensible business attire and the hustle of investments being bought, sold and surreptitiously relocated to offshore accounts, bursting instead with celebrants rejecting all limits of taste and discretion in favor of colors, fabrics, contraptions and devices that expose and conceal body parts in tantalizing combinations. At the end of this mile and a half long procession down Market Street an enormous outdoor plaza of food vendors, live performers, DJs, tents and stages keep the crowd on their feet until exhaustion or the lure of a new party claims their attention.

Of the hordes of visitors filling the motels, hotels, guest rooms and couches throughout the Bay Area and beyond for Pride weekend in 2010 I was responsible for only three. My friend Guinevere arrived on a Friday evening, pulling into our driveway after a three hour trip from her home in a smaller city several hours to the south. She and her two traveling companions exited the car and slid luggage from the trunk. We exchanged embraces on the front porch. As soon as our round of greetings was complete Guinevere sheepishly announced that she and her friends had to leave. They were late for a women's square dance at a nearby nightclub. Daniel and I gave them our permission to leave us for an evening of hay bales, fiddle music and a dance floor full of city cowgirls kicking up their boot heels. We watched from the sidelines as bags were stowed in the guest room, bathrooms were used and apologies reiterated before our guests hurried out the front door and climbed back into the car.

For the next two days I felt like the owner of a boarding house. I didn't realize that three middle-aged women could revert to the fervent energy of their youth without the need for medical intervention. This weekend escape from one of the more conservative cities in California had triggered a tidal wave of activity. I made breakfast each morning, setting toast and coffee in front of my guests as they gathered at the dining room table. They took nibbles of food and sips from their mugs. By the time they'd run out of stories of revelers dressed in wedding gowns, kilts, latex body suits and nothing at all they were awake and eager to pursue their next adventure.

I was both jealous and relieved each morning as they departed. Over the course of two decades I'd rarely missed the opportunity to attend the parade. But the pleasure of a serene summer morning in Oakland, with the birds in our yard collaborating on a medley worthy of a Disney animated film and a warm breeze rustling the morning air, was too beguiling to accept Guinevere's invitation to join them at this massive, crowded event. We waved goodbye as the group drove away, headed towards the BART station and the train that would whisk them into downtown SF. Then Daniel climbed into his own car to shop at a flea market and I went inside.

My first stop was the laundry room. Dirty clothes formed a pyramid-shaped heap on the linoleum floor. I separated several pairs of jeans from the pile and dropped them into the washing machine, then pulled the dryer door open and retrieved a newly dried load. I carried this warm bundle to the kitchen table and spread it across the wooden surface.

Somewhere between applying the final fold to one t-shirt and selecting the next from the jumble a strange sensation passed through me. The feeling of relaxation that had made the morning so serene suddenly shifted into something unsettling. I ran my fingers along the smooth surface of the fabric, perplexed by this contraction in mood.

During the course of the next few minutes this feeling of anxiety blossomed into a state of persistent uneasiness. Contentment was replaced by dread. My heart rate mimicked my distress, climbing upward. I stared at the curtains that fluttered in front of the open window, wondering why this bucolic morning had suddenly become so perilous.

I circled the perimeter of the kitchen, following the contours of the granite-topped island as the anxiety grew stronger, until my agitation pushed me beyond the confines of this small circumference. I hurried out the doors that opened on to the back patio, then followed the brick walkway around the side of the house to the front yard, then ascended the four wooden stairs to the porch and entered the house again. I paced this looping circuit repetitively, treading floor and stone, shade and sunlight, interior and exterior. The world had narrowed to the pounding of my heart and a dizziness that made me wobble as I walked.

My familiarity with panic attacks was limited to performances I'd seen in movies. Trembling, sweating and dizziness were the symptoms that the best actors mimicked with skillful realism. From the audience's point of view these breakdowns are dominated by a loss of physical control. Now I understood that the external signs were the superficial aspects of this disorder. A much more terrifying message dominated my thoughts, undiluted by logic or rationale. I knew I was going to die. I would plunge into unconsciousness from the convulsions of my thundering heartbeat. My heart would fail under the onslaught of this dizzying pulse. The blood vessels that carry oxygen to my brain would rupture under the inexorable pressure.

I clutched my phone, slick with sweat, in my right hand, my forefinger poised above the keypad. Each time I willed myself to press the three numbers that would call 911 a shudder stopped me. I could imagine a siren wailing through nearby streets, the squeal of brakes as the ambulance came to a halt in front of my house, the paramedics leaping from the vehicle. My neighbors would emerge from their houses and gather in groups on the sidewalk, murmuring and whispering. The thought of drawing this maudlin level of attention to myself forced me into even more distraught motion, trying to stay one step ahead of my own collapse.

The early afternoon heat had brought the outdoor temperature to almost 90 degrees and the interior of my house near 80. In between sickening waves of dread I wondered if my anguish was caused by the rising temperature. My house, like tens of thousands of homes in the Bay Area, had no air conditioning system. Daniel and I relied on the breezes that blow in on most summer evening to relieve the oppression of hot days. This was a popular source of cost-free climate control in the Bay Area.

It is also a fickle system that that is subject to the moods of nature. Heat waves can settle over the Bay Area for days, inflicting their harshest effects on the cities that sprawl towards the east and farthest from the ocean's cooling currents. As I paced I wiped sweat from my forehead, trying to rationalize this event as heat exhaustion and not a dire psychological breakdown.

I veered out of my path and turned down the main hallway in our house. In the bathroom I shed my sweaty t-shirt, shorts and underwear. I stepped into the shower and huddled beneath the cold spray of water, curling my toes against the tile. I managed to remain under this chilly spray for several minutes, then I dried myself and put on clean clothes.

I had further remedies in mind. In the kitchen I filled a glass with water and stirred a tablespoon of salt into it, knowing that salt depletion from prolonged sweating in hot weather was a health risk. I drank it in several long gulps, wincing at its briny taste.

I opened a can of chicken soup and spooned it into my mouth, hoping that my disorientation and lightheadedness could be attributed to hunger.

My body's spiral towards heart attack, stroke and death was unchanged by these attempted antidotes. My pulse raced at 170 beats per minute. My fresh t-shirt was already damp with sweat. I tasted the sour burn of salt in the back of my throat. I returned to my peripatetic loop, circling the exterior of the house and passing through the interior.

The sound of car wheels on asphalt jolted me

from my ruminations. I scrambled behind the trunk of the large magnolia tree that spread its canopy over our yard and watched as Guinevere's car came to a stop in our driveway. I could hear laughter as the three occupants exited the vehicle. I stayed in my hiding place, a hideous recluse ashamed to reveal his presence to these vibrant human beings.

Reality had become progressively more distorted as the day shifted from morning to afternoon. Anxiety had transformed the world into a landscape of sharp edges and flattened perspectives. This trio walking towards the front gate resembled caricatures rendered in garish strokes of color. I shuddered at the realization that I had drifted even further away from sanity.

I stepped out of the shadows and walked across the lawn. My smile was an exaggerated display of teeth and gums. I dug my fingernails into the palm of my hand and made a silent vow to maintain eye contact and let my friends lead the conversation.

I tried not to sway as I greeted Guinevere and her friends. I kept my gaze on their faces, laughing when their own grins indicated their amusement, frowning sympathetically when their foreheads wrinkled. Their visual and audio signals were my roadmap to acceptable public behavior.

I successfully feigned mental stability for several minutes, clenching my jaw each time I felt the urge to blurt out that the glancing sunlight made Guinevere's face look like a grinning skull or that my knees were about to buckle. Fortunately Guinevere saved me from a jabbering confession by making her own announcement. She gestured to one of her friends, who had wedged herself into a shadowy corner of the porch like a sinister doll, and explained that she had to be home in three hours for her daughter's birthday party. Guinevere's tone shifted as she admitted that she regretted having barely spent time with me and Daniel. I interrupted her before she could continue her interminable apology. They shouldn't dawdle, I told her, or they would be late. Her friend's daughter needed her mother. I clutched Guinevere to me in a fleeting semblance of a hug. Within minutes my three guests had packed their luggage and were gone.

My encounter with Guinevere and her friends had temporarily distracted me from my failing nerves but now the fear came roaring back. I stepped inside the house and gripped the doorknob, the only stationary object in a room that seemed to be tilting like the deck of a sinking boat.

When Daniel arrived home half an hour later I was in our backyard, seated stiffly upright on a wooden bench we had built halfway up the steep slope. I flung chicken scratch in shaky bursts across the ground, watching our birds peck like mechanical puppets at the gritty mix of dirt and grain. I clamped my trembling hands to my side and suppressed rapid breaths as I accompanied Daniel into the house. He grumbled about the traffic, then brightened as he told me about the box of vintage doll heads he had purchased at a bargain price. I fought the urge to moan like an undead spirit.

When we arrived at the kitchen my façade crumbled. Daniel watched wide-eyed as my hands flew into the air and flapped like frantic birds in front of my face. My attempts to offer an explanation resulted in a garbled string of words. It was an extravagant, disjointed spectacle. In between bouts of hyperventilation I could see the shocked expression on Daniel's face.

He leaned against the counter and directed questions at me, his voice undercut by nervousness. Why did this happen? What had caused it? My panic was feeding his.

I gasped, trying to form a response. I had pondered these questions intently during the first hour of my breakdown and couldn't find an answer.

His voice was shaky as he announced a diagnosis for my condition. I was sweating profusely and the temperature outside was near 90 degrees. My symptoms had lasted for hours. I was suffering from heat exhaustion. He softened his tone. I needed to rest and recover.

I agreed to an enforced period of time on the couch. Daniel placed a kitchen towel packed with ice on my neck and pointed a whirring fan at my body. I clung to a narrow ledge of reality as the sun set and the fading light was replaced by the flickering images of television shows. Surges of panic continued to ebb and flow throughout the evening, right up until the moment I walked down the hallway to the darkened bedroom, slipped beneath the sheets and squeezed my eyelids shut.

My first action when I woke in the morning light was to clamp two fingers to my wrist. Trepidation became relief. My pulse was even and steady. I rose and stood in a room that refused to spin or cause dizziness.

I pressed my bare feet against the hardwood floor and pondered my breakdown from the perspective of a witness to a clinical event. Heat exhaustion was the main culprit, a debilitating physical crisis that had triggered profound waves of anxiety. I could add this day's tribulations to the list of health issues that seemed to pile up like crashed cars on the freeway of life as I grew older. Torn meniscus, herniated disc, high cholesterol, heat exhaustion, panic attack: they were part of an unwanted accumulation. I walked down the hallway towards the kitchen, relishing the domestic morning routine that would start with coffee and end with me climbing into my car to drive to work, determined to relegate this disruption of normal behavior to distant memory.

Chapter 4

Bad bowels can make us weep. The churning of a faulty digestive system turns simple tasks into grueling challenges. We sprint through the grocery store, racing to the finish line. We sit through protracted business meetings in squirming discomfort. We keep a mental map of the nearest bathroom when we are traveling, knowing that we are always just a few feet away from potential humiliation.

The population of microbes that occupy our gastrointestinal tract make our vast planet, teeming with billions of humans, seem like a sparsely occupied wilderness. Trillions of bacteria thrive in the looping coil of digestive organs that wind through our abdomen. The role of intestinal flora in the overall health of the human organism is a new frontier in science. A growing number of researchers have called the human gut our second brain. Its role in the moderation of mood and mental health is the subject of academic journals and studies.

When these bacteria are working in harmony we are content. We can work or travel without fear. We walk to the bathroom instead of racing to it and emerge smiling instead of grimacing. We are proud participants in a productive relationship with our flourishing bacterial partners.

When our intestinal microbiota betray us salty tears fall.

In the summer of 2010 my bowels were operating in a state of insurrection. My stools looked like something you'd find drifting along the edges of a stagnant swamp. I endured this distress with stoic determination, hoping that the passage of time would alleviate my symptoms. I modified my diet to improve my colonic functions. I purchased a ninety-day supply of select probiotics that drained my bank account and needed to be coddled as delicately as hummingbird eggs. I bought digestive enzymes, vitamins and organic herbal supplements that had been harvested by disciples of a guru on a spiritual commune. I increased my intake of fiber, eliminated wheat, ate whole grains and adjusted fats and proteins up and down like they were dyspeptic children on a seesaw.

The symptoms refused to retreat. I searched through hazy memories of my medical history for possible causes of my discomfort. I'd had periods of irritable bowel syndrome on several occasions in my life. My last colonoscopy had occurred at least five years earlier, a length of time I suspected was sufficient to allow malignant lumps to grow and flourish in the walls of my colon. I'd always been prone to hypochondria, ready to attribute any health problem to obscure, deadly diseases whose names and agonizing symptoms I'd committed to memory.

There was an additional element that I knew could be contributing to my intestinal problems, an influence that taunted me as my distress continued.

I was certain that virulent germs had been playing hide and seek in my colon for years or decades, a group of microbial hitchhikers whose debilitating effects had ebbed and waned since occupying my system. They had infected me when I'd traveled in South America in the 1990s, or they had entered my body via food I'd consumed in one of the budget neighborhood restaurants I loved to frequent, or I had been infected by casual contact with a contaminated person. I knew that that there was a biological basis for my condition, not nebulous psychological causes and unknown stress factors.

A visit to my physician both confirmed and countered my concerns. Dr. Wan disagreed with the most alarmist elements of my self-diagnosis but he assented to placing an order for stool tests. A few days later I handed a brown paper bag containing small vials of my feces, shaken and suspended in a swirl of chemicals, to the man at the front desk of the laboratory. He snapped on a pair of latex gloves and plucked the bag from my fingers.

My lab results arrived in my email inbox two days later. I skimmed through the names of microbes displayed like a list of obscure Latin titles in a dusty academic library. Each line terminated with a single conclusive piece of text. I had tested negative for the parasites, amoebas, bacteria and other pathogenic germs that can lodge themselves in our gut.

I had a single question prepared for my follow up call with Dr. Wan. After a polite exchange of greetings I asked him if the tests could be wrong.

I could visualize the cogs in his brain whirring before delivering a response. He explained that there can be a tiny percentage of false negatives. He repeated this statement, emphasizing the word "tiny," then proclaimed his confidence that my test results were accurate.

He continued speaking before I could interject my own comments. Our digestive tract is subject to the influence of our autonomic nervous system, he told me. This new flare-up of irritable bowel syndrome that I was experiencing was a perfect example of the role that stress can play in the physiological process. He chuckled, an unexpected injection of levity into his earnest tone, as he told me that the quality of our excrement can relate directly to the quality of our thoughts.

I told him that the tests yielded one result but my stomach revealed another. I asked Dr. Wan if there was medication that would eradicate any germs that may have eluded the lab tests, regardless of how slim the odds. I bolstered my request with a simple argument. If a round of medication failed to improve the functions of my digestive tract then I would know that stress was the culprit. I would be motivated enough to pursue the relaxation techniques – deep breathing exercises, meditation, yoga - that I resisted.

I was surprised when Dr. Wan agreed to my request. He paused before explaining that this would be a form of empirical study, eliminating possible pathogens through a controlled process. He told me there was one common broad-spectrum drug used to treat intestinal microbes. He would order it for me to pick up at the pharmacy that afternoon.

Flagyl is the brand name for the generic drug metronidazole. When I removed the first pill from the bottle that evening I could feel its bulk in the palm of my hand. It was shaped like a miniature torpedo, with a thick girth and an elliptical shape. I filled a glass of water and placed the pill in my mouth. During the brief moment that it made contact with my tongue I could feel my throat constrict. I hurriedly gulped water, trying to flood this foreign object straight into my stomach.

In that moment, leaning against the kitchen counter, trying to clear the nauseating taste from my mouth, I established a flawed precedent. There's a reason that our hand recoils when we grab the scorching handle of an iron frying pan or that we freeze in fear when we encounter a coiled snake on a rocky trail. My body was trying to repel this potentially toxic intruder. I should have spit it into the sink and dissolved it under a stream of water.

Instead I choked it down. A popular adage resonated through my mind: the more bitter the medicine, the better its results. This gag-inducing drug would shrivel the toughest microbes in my intestines. I vowed to follow the prescribed dosage of one pill, three times a day, for seven days duration.

Five days after ingesting the first of these pills I gingerly lowered myself into a chair at our dining room table and unfolded a sheaf of papers. These were the printed instructions that had been enclosed with the metronidazole. I had discarded them in a drawer, disinterested in so much excessive information. Now I ran my forefinger across the lines, squinting at the text.

The two page list of side effects was an homage to human suffering. Metronidazole can cause diarrhea or constipation, fatigue or nervousness, somnolence or insomnia. You might feel flushed with heat or chilled by cold. You might have tingling or numbness. Our physical reaction to tossing these pills into your mouth is as easy to predict as the outcome of flinging a pair of dice down a craps table at a Las Vegas casino.

I creased the pages into a small square and flicked it to the floor. My hostility towards this list wasn't predicated by the symptoms that were included, but by those that were omitted. What about side effects that don't fit into the normal range. What about bizarre and disorienting? What about dissociative and debilitating? Flagyl is proven to eradicate bacterial infections but the risk of mental disturbance is just as real. It had tapped into the same subconscious vein of anxiety that had caused me to experience a day of panic two months earlier, but with much more heightened perception. Paranoia was a constant companion. Sleep was a twilight of restless eye movements accompanied by dreams so vivid I had to yell into the darkened bedroom to dispel phantom forms and figures. I woke each morning in the same state of agitation that had accompanied me to bed the night before. The effects of metronidazole were more like a traumatic hallucinogenic trip than a curative treatment.

I went into the bathroom, picked up the prescription bottle and tilted it over the toilet. A cluster of the pills teetered at the rim, poised to tumble into a watery grave. Then I flipped the bottle upright and set it on the countertop. I envisioned a guerilla outpost of parasites barricaded in a recessed pocket of my intestines. They were seething, vile creatures, plotting subjugation of all native organisms. I would be debilitated by anxiety if I failed to complete all seven days of medication. I placed one of the pills on my tongue and washed it down with a glass of water, fighting the urge to gag.

I went to bed that evening weak with nausea but clinging to the hope that the end of this anguish was only two days way.

At 3:00 AM I opened my eyes. The room was a wash of silvery moonlight and shadows etched across the floor and walls. I floundered in confusion, trying to adjust to this jarring leap from sleep to consciousness without the grace of transition. I was sitting bolt upright in bed, my legs extended before me.

I walked down the hallway. My head felt like it was floating behind me. I leaned against the sink in our kitchen and let my shoulders go slack. I felt as leaden as the pale appliances that loomed in the darkness around me.

This was the night that depression permeated my mind and body. It had been lurking at the periphery of my existence since my arrival into adulthood decades ago, a vexing but aloof presence. I had no strength to combat its arrival.

Logic would dictate that a grown man who has lived through multiple decades on this turbulent planet would have encountered almost every form of sorrow that life can deliver. I'd been present as each of my parents had reached the ends of their lives. I'd struggled with the heartache and anger that comes with failed relationships. I'd soaked up enough grim news and social media outrage, lies, truths and distortions to know that fairness and justice are concepts dangled like existential carrots just beyond our reach.

But this pain was unprecedented. I had no reference for it. My brain was in the grips of an immobilizing force. I had passed beyond thought, emotion and comprehension into a state of pure mental torment.

A sinuous thought unraveled in the midst of this anguish, a revelation so startling that I could feel my body shiver. It relayed a simple truth. Death is the most logical alternative to extreme suffering. It is a dire choice and it is a last choice, but it is the only choice.

I walked back down the hallway into the bathroom and gently slid the door closed behind me to avoid waking Daniel, asleep in the adjacent bedroom. I swung the mirrored medicine chest open. Several prescription bottles lined the top shelf. My eyes gravitated to one located in the far corner.

These were Seroquel pills, in 25mg doses. They had been prescribed to me to counter the anxiety that had gradually been creeping into my life. I had taken one pill, once. That single dose had plunged me into a state of twilight sedation for hours, laying prone on the couch, incapacitated by muscles that had the pliancy of soft rubber until the haze had eventually lifted.

I opened the bottle. The sight of the small orange pills heaped to the rim triggered a rush of adrenaline. The solution to my mental agony was right in front of me. It would wait patiently on the shelf for my return. I placed the bottle back in its spot among the row of containers and swung the medicine chest door shut.

I could hear Daniel's light snore as I slid into bed next to him. An image of the bottle of pills, lit by a pale glow, shimmered in the blank canvas behind my eyelids. The lid would lift away with a tug of my fingers. The pills would spill into my palm. They would slide, aided by sips of water, down my throat and into my stomach where they would dissolve into my bloodstream and drag me into sedation, then unconsciousness, then cessation of breath and heartbeat. This knowledge allowed me to drift into sleep that night.

When I woke several hours later I had gone through a reverse metamorphosis. I'd shed all color, vitality and motion. I could feign normalcy, but I was removed from the world around me. I was enveloped in a dense cocoon.

All my rituals that morning were artifice. I poured coffee into my mug and sipped the warm liquid but it had no flavor. Our two dogs wagged their tails and circled us, reminding us of our eternal obligation to feed them, pet them and love them, but now they were objects without purpose. I spooned bites of breakfast cereal into my mouth, chewing a substance with the texture of sodden cardboard.

I forced a rasp in my throat and told Daniel that I was going to stay home from work. He cocked his head and watched me as I averted my eyes and counted the pieces of cereal bobbing on the milky surface in my bowl.

Was I feeling OK? he asked.

Fine, I said, shrugging.

I thought my performance was a convincing portrayal of a husband with a sore throat on a workday morning. Daniel's widening eyes revealed the failure of my performance. I could sense his growing alarm that we were heading into another round of the panic and anxiety that had consumed me so recently.

I crossed the floor and spread my arms across the sleek granite surface of the kitchen island and gripped its rounded edges, trying to gather this monolithic object into an embrace. The smooth surface of the polished stone was cool against my cheek.

I could hear Daniel's voice buzzing in my ear like an aggravated mosquito. Are you having a panic attack? he asked.

You should get ready for work, I murmured. Tears dampened the space between my flesh and the stone.

Daniel hunched his upper body over mine, trying to hug me at an angle that defied logistics. We were two players in an impassioned game of Twister.

He tugged at my shoulder and told me to get my phone and wallet. He was going to drive me to the psychiatric clinic that our health provider operated near downtown Oakland.

My movements were sullen as I trudged through the house, sliding keys and wallet into my pockets, slipping on shoes and a jacket. I resented Daniel's intrusion into my lethal ruminations. Suicide is a party of one and he had crashed an exclusive guest list. I kept my eyes averted as he accompanied me through the front door and to the car.

Twenty minutes later, we walked through the entrance of the mental health clinic. We passed beige walls and gray chairs offset by bright abstract paintings that seemed incongruous among the bland colors around them.

We followed the narrow strip of plastic laid across the carpet like a trampled version of the yellow brick road, guiding us to the two receptionists at the front counter. Several people were waiting in line ahead of us. The two clerks seemed stuck in slow-motion repetition, sliding clipboards across the counter to clients, swiping payment cards, answering questions.

My steps were tentative when we reached the front of the line and the clerk beckoned Daniel and me forward. I put my elbows on the countertop and leaned in towards the man seated behind his computer. I could see the striations of brown and blue that ran through the irises of his eyes.

How can I help you? he asked.

I stared to my right. The first row of chairs in the waiting room were located less than six feet away. The scattering of people seated closest to where I stood would find perverse pleasure in eavesdropping on the mental breakdown of the man at the counter next to them.

The receptionist repeated the question. Can I Help You?

I opened my mouth and a few strangled words

escaped my lips.

The man's eyebrows twitched like two antennae sensing a disturbance in the air. He leaned forward. Are you having a crisis? he asked. His formal expression had transformed into watchful concern.

The room seemed to lurch sideways and I clutched the counter. I had struggled all morning to find a name for this stark collapse of reality and perception. This clerk had, with one simple word, identified my condition. I was in a crisis. I was drowning in a maelstrom of despondence and dissociation. Crisis was the precise definition for my state of mind.

I nodded, a motion so short that I was surprised when the clerk returned his own gesture of acknowledgement.

Three minutes later, Daniel and I were seated in the waiting room. I gripped a clipboard in in my left hand and a ballpoint pen, slick with sweat from my palm, in my right. I fumbled through the questionnaire, marking boxes. This printed sheet was a standardized form for providing therapists and psychiatrists with a snapshot of the mental health of their client. They covered nearly every imaginable form of human behavior and emotion. Eating habits, sleep cycles and mood swings were all curiosities that could be rated on a scale from never to always, mild to extreme, occasionally to frequently.

The final question on the form loomed at the bottom of the page. It was printed in large, bold type framed by a bordered box that commanded attention.

Did I have a plan for harming myself or ending my life?

I slumped deeper into my chair then pressed the tip of the pen against the paper and heard the loud scratch as I marked the box yes.

Daniel and I waited for fifteen minutes before Dr. Friant appeared in a doorway and called my name. I rose and followed him. He stayed several steps ahead of me as he led the way down the long hallway to his office.

The doctor halted before one of the doors and ushered me through it. His office was a study in subdued masculinity. Dark polished furniture mingled with wide leafy plants that grazed the ceiling. I lowered myself onto a leather sofa in one corner of this tame jungle as the doctor seated himself in an easy chair directly across from me.

His first question was one I've answered in therapists' offices throughout Northern California over the course of decades. During my life I've plunged into psychotherapy for short periods of time and for extended durations. These cycles started in my college years and continue to this day. It is a process that is both routine and unique each time I walk into my first appointment with a new psychotherapist.

Why are you here today? Dr. Friant asked.

In the past I relied on a standard response. I think I'm depressed, I would say, but I'm not sure. This statement may have sounded glib but in fact it was genuine. I had no suicidal thoughts or urges. I wasn't stricken by hopelessness or deep despair. I was functional in my relationships and work. I never sat slumped on a couch, head cradled in my hands, while a bleak soundtrack played in the background, the stereotypical portrayal of depression as depicted by TV commercials and television dramas.

Yet, something dark and disturbing had nagged at me for as long as I could remember. I regarded suffering and dread as fundamental elements of existence. I woke during the night and tallied war, poverty, homelessness, violence and brutality the way that most insomniacs count sheep.

Throughout the procession of therapists and counselors that have dotted the timeline of my life none had ever diagnosed me as chronically or clinically depressed. My health and my life were never at risk. None ever recommended medication or expressed concern about me being a danger to myself or others.

In that moment, while Dr. Friant watched me from his leather chair, I knew that my answer was permanently altered.

I opened my mouth to explain how the world around me had transformed from a stable and predictable environment into a merciless dystopia. I listened with a mix of dread and horror as an ethereal, keening wail rose from deep in my chest, piercing the soothing ambience of Dr. Friant's office. I squeezed my eyes shut and willed it to stop.

My break from reality grew deeper and wilder. The stream of unearthly sounds was compounded by a series of humiliating grunts. Tears dribbled from my eyes. My breakdown had all the hallmarks of the deep grief that humans express over the death or departure of a loved one, but the object of my pain wasn't another person. I was sobbing for myself. All feeling of hope receded beyond any horizon line. The intangible force that feeds a person's will to live had been extinguished in me.

Dr. Friant maintained a calm gaze as I struggled to regain control of my emotions and my body.

Have you made any plans to harm yourself ? he asked.

I nodded and told him yes. A new surge of liquid leaked from my nose and eyes.

Dr. Friant leaned forward in his chair, cleared his throat and explained that he was committing me to a psychiatric facility for a minimum of 72 hours, where I would be treated for depression and anxiety.

Chapter 5

There is no separate admittance room for new patients arriving at the Sheldon Psychiatric Facility in Oakland, CA. The two paramedics wheel you on a gurney through the double-hinged doors. They nod at the uniformed security guard who acknowledges them with a grunt of familiarity then shifts his gaze to the new client entering the facility. The paramedics bring the gurney to a stop in front of the nurse's station and you push yourself upward from your reclined position. You don't know it, but you've stepped into a spotlight. A dozen or more pairs of eyes have turned towards you, their attention diverted from the chattering television, strewn magazines and conversations that keep the residents in the adjacent community room occupied. They watch you as you swing your feet to the floor. Your clothes are rumpled and your face is gaunt from the compounded indignities of mental crisis, prolonged emergency room detention and ambulance travel.

Their curiosity is the reflexive response of any group of people assessing a new arrival into their territory. Your gender, clothes, race, weight and age are the physical characteristics that intrigue them, but there is another guessing game going on in the minds of this watchful jury. They want to know what aberrant behavior has brought you through these doors. It is the answer that each resident will covertly or bluntly try to glean from you once you start mingling with your new gathering of roommates.

The community room exists in a state of chronic tension, hovering between simmering boredom and restless agitation. The room is large enough to seem spacious but feels constricted by the absence of windows. It is illuminated by fluorescent lights and opens to hallways that lead to other areas of the facility. Green vinyl chairs line the perimeter. Patients change seating locations as frequently as they change moods. Late afternoon brings the official advent of the stream of television news, sports, talk shows and sitcoms that placates a shifting crowd of viewers.

I stood next to the gurney waiting for instructions from one of the nurses or attendants busily consulting computer screens or engaged in telephone calls behind the front counter. I felt like a marionette with half his strings cut, drawing on deep reserves of strength to remain upright. I'd been in transition for almost eight hours, starting with my arrival at the mental health clinic early that morning then progressing to a five hour stay in a hospital emergency room while they sought, and found, an open bed for me in a psychiatric facility.

A voice in my left ear startled me. I turned and made eye contact with a woman wearing a blue polo shirt and jeans. Her badge, dangling from a lanyard around her neck, identified her as Mona, a nursing assistant.

My new chaperone led me to a small room lined with wooden counters. Crayons, sketchbooks, acrylic paints and an assortment of other art supplies were stacked along the walls. We sat at one of tables and Mona opened a file folder while I propped my elbows on the tabletop.

Her questions prompted gruff responses from me. This was the third time that day that I'd had my moods, thoughts and behaviors probed by psychiatrists and medical professionals. I grumbled as I dredged up rote answers to queries that now seemed redundant and irritating.

Fortunately Mona was experienced with the fatigue that affected new arrivals. She made an efficient dash through several forms, jotting my answers. Ten minutes after we sat she clicked her ballpoint pen and told me she would take me to my room.

We retraced our original route through the building and came to a stop in front of one of a dozen doors that were spaced evenly along a wide hallway. I stepped across the threshold and let my eyes adapt to the dim light. When the details sharpened my eyes dampened with frustration.

The long rectangular room was barren and bleak. It was occupied by two twin beds, each flanked by a spindly nightstand. That was the sum of the furnishings. No decor adorned any surface. Lamps, curtains, mirrors, art, cords, hangers or any other potential tools for suicide were banished. Sunlight blasted the room during the day and yellow halogen light poured into the room at night through a single window without curtains or blinds. Sheldon had created an environment that was physically safe but desolate of comfort or reassurance.

Mona showed no awareness of my teary disappointment as she led me back to the community room where she gestured for me to occupy any chair. I dropped into one that was sufficiently distant from any nearby occupant. At this late hour the staff had reduced the lighting to half of its daytime brilliance. The large room had become the refuge of those patients waiting for their racing thoughts to diminish and their medications to initiate the sleepy shuffle down the hallway to bed. I avoided eye contact with the few people still scattered around the room.

Nothing in my natural time clock led me to the decision that I was ready for sleep that evening, despite my exhaustion and the digital numbers on the nurse's clock reminding me that the evening was advancing deeper into night. 9:30, 10:00 then 10:30 appeared on the glowing screen. Depression combined with anxiety is a diabolical union. Our despair makes us want to retreat from the world while our nervousness forces us into a state of jittery anticipation as we try to postpone any encounter with the gallery of psychic apparitions that wait behind our eyelids in darkened bedrooms.

When the clock silently announced 11:00 PM I walked to my assigned room and slid beneath the bedspread. My mind promptly fell into a game of sadistic mental leapfrog. Each bleak new thought jumped nimbly ahead of its companions to repeat sharp recriminations against my behavior, personality and existence. I was a burden to everyone. I had dragged my husband, my friends, my relatives and my co-workers into the morass of my emotional turmoil and drama. I had forced these genial hospital attendants, who earned survival wages watching over a herd of unstable, demanding patients, to clean up the mess of my failure. The message was grinding and tenacious. I was despicable and I was useless. My departure from this world would be my gift to all.

The door to the brightly lit hallway remained ajar the entire night. Every half hour an attendant would step into the room to make sure that my roommate and I were still in our beds and our chests were still rising and falling in the universal rhythm that indicates life. After hours of fitful dozing, waking repeatedly to the looming figure of a man or woman standing at the foot of my bed, making a notation on a clipboard, I realized that this austere room served a special purpose. It was where new patients passed their first night under heightened observation for suicidal risk.

My roommate was a lump sheathed in a blanket on the adjacent bed. Periodically he would shift in his sleep and then become motionless again. I saw him rise once, late in the night, and shuffle into the bathroom, clutching the blanket around his body. He was a young man, wearing a black t-shirt and white boxer shorts. I would later learn that he had swallowed a bottle of Xanax and had regained consciousness in the ICU unit of a San Francisco hospital. The vestiges of the drug, plus a heavy dose of a mood stabilizer, put him into a deep sleep for almost 24 hours.

Sheldon Inc. understood the importance of imposing a regimented schedule on a population wracked by internal anarchy. The day would begin at 6:30 a.m. with the sharp rap of knuckles against our bedroom doors and the announcement that breakfast was ready. Dragging ourselves out of bed in response to this disruption wasn't mandatory, but it was recommended. The attendants performed some of the most basic and unrewarding tasks on the ward—monitoring us while we shaved in front of the bathroom mirror, hovering outside the tiled stall while we showered, ushering us into the outdoor area for an hour each day—but they also held a strategic power that trumped the authority of the registered nurses doling out medications or the executives in distant company headquarters remotely managing their chain of health care facilities.

The attendants would engage the patients in

casual conversations throughout the day. These interactions were seemingly spontaneous and casual. How did you sleep? How's your appetite? How's your energy level? Are you getting along with the other residents? New patients might be charmed by the attention or annoyed by the intrusion but we tended to respond with candor.

My first encounter occurred the day after my arrival as I paced from one end of the long main hallway and back again. I kept my gaze on the floor as I walked, barely noticing my surroundings.

I almost bumped into a stationary object directly in my path. I looked up to see an attendant named Conrad standing directly in front of me. He spoke before I could step around him

How was I feeling? he asked. He had a warm smile.

I told him I was going to lie down in my room until I could think of a good reason to get up again.

He nodded genially, undeterred by my sarcasm, and reminded me there was a stretching class in ten minutes and an art workshop later that day. I told him I wasn't interested and continued my forward motion.

These frank responses blurted by fledgling

arrivals tended to shift soon after we were admitted to the facility. Veteran patients would lean towards newcomers and whisper that these impromptu conversations had a more covert purpose than their innocent guise suggested. Our answers didn't dissipate into irrelevance after we parted ways with a friendly attendant. The clipboards they held, carried alongside their hips like six-shooters, were their tools for recording and monitoring our moods and behaviors. The notes they jotted would be passed along to the doctors who oversaw our progress.

My psychiatrist was assigned to me by the invisible hand of the hospital administration. Dr. Aldred would arrive every other afternoon, a large man dressed in an outfit of black slacks, pressed shirt, dark tie and buffed black shoes. His professional appearance contrasted sharply with the casual outfits worn by a staff of employees who performed their long work shifts on their feet and in constant motion.

We had our first session in a small office reserved for clinicians. Dr. Aldred's physical bulk seemed to diminish behind the heavy oak desk that occupied almost a third of the room. His head bobbed while he talked, a signal that he was paying attention to my words while he jotted notes in my file. He saw a steady succession of patients during his afternoons on the ward, a parade of men and women diagnosed with unipolar depression, bipolar disorder, delusional thinking, schizophrenia and an encyclopedic array of other mental illnesses. His job was to manage these clients as efficiently as possible, analyzing each one for disorders that could hopefully be improved with the right combination of medication, hospitalization, therapy and luck.

During the fifteen minutes that I sat in the chair across from the doctor I spoke with an honesty that veered too far into the realm of indiscretion. It was a practice that I would quickly revise.

I explained how my depression had distilled itself into a single toxic essence. Suicidal ideation was no longer a part of a larger tapestry of symptoms. My fixation on death now defined the entire disease. My eyes glinted with the passion of a preacher too deeply swayed by his own sermon as I told Dr. Aldred that this state of mind brought a welcome degree of clarity to my turbulent thoughts. It muted the profound guilt I felt over my selfish, destructive plans.

Dr. Aldred's head halted halfway through one of its motions. The only sound in the room was the hum of the air conditioning system operating somewhere deep within the hospital. He narrowed his eyes and told me that introversion and social isolation are exceptionally dangerous behaviors for a person experiencing profound suicidal ideation. An isolated person will become increasingly susceptible to their most destructive thoughts. He insisted that I place myself in group settings each day and that I engage in conversations with patients and staff members. He told me to attend the mindfulness class and the workshops. He prescribed an antidepressant, the first I'd ever taken, to be administered starting that evening. He fixed his gaze on me for ten unwavering seconds then repeated these mandates again.

I left the session both resentful and respectful of the doctor's advice. My decades of living with an awareness of depression had taught me the validity of his demands. Solitude had always been a compelling fantasy for me. Dreamy scenarios of moving to a remote ranch in New Mexico or a rustic cabin in Maine had regularly intruded on the clamor of my youthful years in San Francisco. During those periods of time that I did experience isolation, in my studio apartment on long weekends with no plans, no money and no available friends, or during solo trips to nearby hiking trails where nature's stillness sometimes bore down with the weight of an ominous, invisible force, a form of mental paralysis would consume me. The importance of social interaction was always a nagging awareness in the back of my mind.

I also knew, from my recent plunge into a major depressive episode, the flaw that undermined the doctor's advice. Suicidal depression is a spiteful culprit. It coerces us into believing that there is only one solution for terminating the pain that it inflicts. Progress, hope and pleasure are not options. Defying or even doubting this assailing message can be a nearly impossible task for a person already disabled by its manipulative presence.

My decision to comply with the doctor's directive that I mingle more and ruminate less was as much a response to his position within the hospital hierarchy as to his professional skills. He had the power to decide if I could leave the institution or would remain for further evaluation. By law we were detainees of the state of California. Section 5150 of the California Welfare and Institutions Code allows the state to hold any person against their will for up to 72 hours if a mental health professional or agent of the law determines they are a danger to themselves or to another person. When that time period has passed a psychiatrist can release the person, ask them to voluntarily stay for further treatment, or extend their involuntary detention. Dr. Aldred's signature on a release form was the key that would allow me to walk out of this sealed environment.

On the morning after my psychiatric session I dutifully rolled out of bed and joined the other sleepy patients straggling towards the cafeteria. We would sip coffee the color of pale brown water and lift forkfuls of scrambled eggs into our mouths while shaking off the effects of last night's medication. The forced intimacy of a confined environment was the perfect medium for accelerated social interaction. We were a collection of different races, genders, religions, politics and sexual orientations, but we had a unique bond. Mental illness kept our community in sticky cohesion. I didn't have to do anything more than make eye contact and start a sentence to initiate a brief or prolonged conversation with most of my fellow residents.

An arsenal of pharmaceuticals was the hospital's weapon against the perilous levels of internal pressure created by our brooding awareness that every door to the outside world was locked. Bottles and boxes of drugs lined the shelves of the medication room. The sharp click of the deadbolt being retracted each morning and evening was like the opening bell at the horse races. Patients milled in the community room while nurses emerged from this vault of precious compounds, each carrying a tray dotted with small plastic cups containing pills and liquids. These staff members would pass through the room like waiters at a catered party, delivering medications after double checking our wrist bands for identification. Most of us received a sedative among the pills that we tossed back with a swallow of water.

Our glum resentment at being denied control over the terms and conditions of our custody was partially alleviated by the visitors that were allowed to join us five evenings a week. The uniformed guard would take up his station by front entrance and keep steady watch as the small crowd of family members and friends surged inward, making sure that no rogue patient swam against the stream, slipping off to freedom. Our institution would, for a few minutes, lose its dystopian sheen. The calm voices of these outsiders were a panacea to the rollercoaster of emotions that the residents rode each day.

When visiting hour commenced I would spot Daniel in the arriving throng and wave at him to follow me. We'd hurry to one of the smaller rooms at the end of the hall and claim a table for ourselves, arriving ahead of the other families and patients seeking their own small island of privacy.

Our conversations never strayed far from innocuous topics. We both knew that benign discussions about movies, neighbors, pets, weather, food and other topics that could be easily summarized in a few pithy comments were a safe alternative to the despair that gripped me the remaining hours of each day.

Forty-five minutes after the start of visiting hours our conversation would be interrupted by the booming voice of an attendant announcing departure time. The visitors would trickle out the door and for one prolonged minute the hallways and rooms would be silent. Then the asylum would belong to the inmates again and the voices of patients and garrulous television hosts would ring off the walls.

During my first day in the psychiatric facility I avoided contact with my fellow residents and our omniscient attendants. I paced the hallways or ate my meals with my eyes averted.

On day two I succumbed to the doctor's mandate for social activity and slid into a vinyl chair in the corner of the community room. I kept my gaze directed towards the linoleum floor.

The sound of angry voices made me look up. On the far side of the room several people were yelling at each other. A tall, chubby man had stepped in front of the television, blocking the view of a group of patients seated in chairs and couches in front of the glowing screen. I couldn't see the flickering images but I could hear a sportscaster's rapid patter.

This bellicose interloper was demanding that the channel be changed to the news. A woman stood facing him, her decibel level matching his. Disgruntled mutterings among the seated viewers exacerbated the volume. The man reminded the woman that it was time for the evening news. She told him that the game would be finished any moment then it would be his turn. She pushed her chin a few inches from his, challenging him to respond.

Those of us sitting along the perimeters of the community room watched as the antagonist spun around and marched away from his adversary. A ruddy sheen had spread across his cheeks and forehead.

I felt a grip of panic when I realized that this deranged man was marching straight towards me. I had no time to make an escape. The empty chair next to me was the focal point of his beeline. He dropped into it with a grunt.

My mind frantically toggled between the options available to me. Both of them were bad. If I pushed myself to my feet and walked away I might trigger his predatory instincts and become the victim of a second verbal assault. If I stayed I would be his human toy to torment. I leaned forward, trying to block his outline in my peripheral vision.

Then he turned towards me and started talking. I glanced furtively in his direction, expecting to see the writhing head of a Hydra, and was startled by his transformation. His eyes had cooled from beacons of rage to calm pools of blue. His feverish complexion had paled. He spoke in a fast, unbroken monotone.

His name was Carl. This was his fourth stay at Sheldon. In a ritual that he repeated almost annually he would reject the lithium and adjunct medications that he took to control his bipolar disorder. His disgust at the apathy, weight gain and haze of forgetfulness caused by this cocktail of drugs became unbearable. He would flush the pills down the toilet in silent glee, then he would stare in the mirror at the overweight man in his mid-forties with a face deeply creased by a lifetime of perpetual anxiety and erratic behavior. He would vow to exercise, quit smoking, practice deep breathing, love his wife and kids more deeply and force this disease into submission.

His wife always rescued him from the ensuing psychotic break. She had lived through these periods of rebellion before. Her request to have him committed to Sheldon, made in conjunction with his psychiatrist, always resulted in an extended stay.

Everyone needs a best prison buddy, and for the next several days Carl became mine. We had personalities that functioned in a strained but effective counterpoint. He was extroverted and I was reserved. He was volatile and I was restrained. He was confrontational and I avoided conflict. We spent hours in each other's company, sitting side by side in the community room. He offered me a ringside view of his angry skirmishes on the playing field and I offered him a safe place on the sidelines.

Jessica was the patient whose presence haunted me the most. She was a poster child for severe mental illness. She was young, pretty and suffered from paranoid schizophrenia. Any person watching her approach from the far end of the hospital's long main hallway, moving with light, fluid steps, would be impressed by her appearance. She was tall and willowy; a lithe, attractive figure dressed in jeans, t-shirt and sneakers. Only when she arrived into close proximity of the viewer did this impression take a disarming turn. Her eyes were set in hollow sockets ashen with dark circles. Her skin was stretched like taut film across jutting cheekbones. The first time she engaged me in a conversation I felt a shock of disorientation. She sat on the arm of the chair where I was slouched, stared into my eyes, and asked me if the doctors required her to be pregnant to leave this facility. There was no caprice in her question, only the trembling fear caused by this tyrannical demand. On another occasion she put her lips to my ear and asked me if the bones in her face were made of plastic. I always managed to respond that her concerns were unfounded. After each encounter I felt a shudder of relief that my mental disease had none of the terrifying hallucinatory aspects that consumed her so deeply.

Jessica was lucky. Sheldon mandated that a patient could only be discharged into a home environment that offered the fundamental elements of practical and emotional support. Our destination might be a house, it might be a mobile home or a cramped apartment, but it would provide a roof over our head, a bed to sleep in, food in the kitchen and a group of friends and relatives pledged to contribute to the stability of the struggling patient.

These requirements gave the residents of Sheldon only a tenuous feeling of confidence. Our hospitalization was a conspicuous reminder of the precarious nature of mental illness. Major depression, bipolar disorder, schizophrenia, dissociative disorders and all the mental diseases that ebb, flow, spike and recede can sabotage the stability of a secure home in an instant. Our safety net was in place, but it could rip or fail at any time.

Almost everyone in the modern world is witness to these failures. When we are walking on a busy city sidewalk, caught up in a pedestrian throng, speed is the priority. We are late for work, late for a meeting, hurrying to get to the subway, hurrying to get home. One of the few obstacles that can stall our momentum is the presence of a person planted like an obstacle in our path. Our instinct for safety will override the competitive urge to stay one step ahead of our marching neighbor. The river of humanity will part and flow around this human impediment. We catch a glimpse of matted hair, stiff with grime, and skin the color of scorched leather.

These messengers from the dark side of humanity say and do the things that test our limits of tolerance. They ramble about bodily functions in such graphic detail that we are both offended and curious. They dig greasy food from Styrofoam containers and chew the remnants with gaping mouths. They curse relatives, celebrities, politicians, cartoon characters and invisible friends equally in sprees of free association. They are a jarring mix of stand-up comedian and grotesque maniac.

Frequently we will hear them before we see them. The machine gun bursts of harsh laughter and the drone of an unbroken monologue are audio signals that cut through the din of traffic, construction equipment and cell phone conversations.

Some of us frown, some of us recoil, some snicker in amusement as we hurry past this agitated, gesticulating figure. Usually we wish they would disappear. They are an inconvenience. They are dangerous. During our moments of visceral reaction it's hard to remember that a human being lies beneath the filthy façade. Like us, they live in the city that we call home, where we breathe the collective air of urban life. We need them as much as they need us. They are a reminder of the complexity and inequity of humanity and the need to apply a critical lens to our perceptions. We offer them, hopefully, a chance to find the treatment that will provide a modicum of relief from their demons and delirium.

Jessica was a long-term resident of Sheldon. Her mental illness was still too unresolved to allow her to return to her parents' house and their vigilant care. My stay would be much briefer. Several days after arriving at Sheldon I had my second meeting with Dr. Aldred. His look of stern admonition was gone as he browsed through recent notes provided by the attendants. Apparently I'd been hitting the right marks in my daily routine. I'd stretched in group classes and journaled in workshops. I'd immersed myself in the cloistered drama of the community room. My personal hygiene reflected my improvement: combed hair, brushed teeth, shaved face. The doctor's response was both a question and a pronouncement when he looked at me and said that I seemed to have made noticeable progress.

I nodded. His presumption of progress was correct. The harshest aspects of my major depressive episode had diminished by a small but perceptible amount. I'd managed to create distance between myself and incessant suicidal ideation. I'd gone from isolation to socialization. The doctor told me that logic pointed to my return home soon. The unspoken context of this proposal was hard to miss. Stable patients needed to be rotated out of the facility as promptly as possible to make room for the abundant supply of new clients waiting in clinics and emergency rooms throughout the Bay Area for an open bed.

The room was stuffy but I felt a chill pass through me. My house had been the setting for my deepest despondency. Every square foot of it was a reminder of the psychic crash that had toppled my belief system and amplified the troubling disconnect between my husband and me. The doctor's offer was both a gift and a threat.

I explained to Dr. Aldred my fear of returning to the site of my breakdown. I expected him to launch into a persuasive argument on the importance of home life as part of the healing process. I was startled to see him nodding in agreement. He told me that the physical location of a psychic trauma can create strong negative associations. He explained that I could leave the hospital and move to a transitional group home. This new facility would provide me with my own bedroom and several housemates, also in transition from psychiatric care to stable living environments. Staff members would continue to monitor and administer medication. A psychotherapist and a psychiatrist would provide periodic sessions with the residents. He would like me to stay there for at least five days.

The following evening, when the community room became the drowsy limbo where patients loitered before departing to their bedrooms, I said goodbye to several of my fellow residents. We stood in front of the nurse's station making droll predictions about our ability to return to the world of jobs, relationships, routine and pervasive stress. We shared a series of hugs that ranged from an awkward pat on the shoulder delivered by a gaunt woman whose name I forgot but whose shy kindness I remembered, to a bone crushing squeeze from Carl who assured me that I would be a success in the outside world. When this group turned back towards the community room I felt a sharp pang of loneliness followed by a rush of relief. My residency in this turbulent environment had ended. The future was once again a wavering line on the horizon.

Chapter 6

I arrived at my new accommodations with my fists clenched tight and my forehead beaded with sweat. My driver was a young woman who swerved her way from Oakland to Fremont nearly oblivious to white lines, speed limits, guardrails or nearby cars. I opened the door of her fifteen-year old Toyota Corolla and inhaled the night air. It was almost 9:00 PM when we pulled into the driveway of Beacon House but the front walkway was blasted by the glare of an industrial-sized overhead light. A small white dog barked furiously behind the wrought iron fence that marked the border of the adjacent house, racing back and forth in a blur. My chaperone turned the knob of the front door and paused to assure me that my new home would be awesome. I nodded and took another gulp of air, grateful to have survived the journey.

The foyer had been reduced to half its original

width by a row of bulky metal filing cabinets pushed against one wall. We took several steps further towards the interior and arrived at cluster of desks, chairs and shelves gathered together to form a makeshift office. Computer monitors were wedged among piles of paperwork. I looked beyond this island of administrative equipment and could see the remainder of the house. There was an open kitchen flanked by a large dining table and, beyond that, a living room with three couches grouped around a television hanging on a wall.

The setting was strangely nostalgic. This was a classic 1970s suburban tract home, with high ceilings and an open floor plan that had once—many decades earlier—offered upwardly mobile buyers the opportunity to own a piece of breezy California lifestyle. I had grown up in a house from a similar era and had passed hours and days in the company of my friends who lived in these homes. Like many of the sprawling real estate developments built during that time period, this neighborhood had suffered through a series of economic downturns without corresponding recovery. I sensed it as we drove through the residential streets that had led to this doorway and could see it in the rooms in front of me. The neglect of decades of frugal maintenance and budget repairs was apparent.

There was only one person on staff at this late evening hour, a young man who turned away from a computer screen and rose to greet me. His scruffy beard and thick hair blended into each other like two thatches of creeping plant life. He gestured for me to sit next to his desk. I felt a dull ache of humiliation as I lowered myself into his chair. Two kids at least a quarter of a century younger than me were now in charge of my life. I had faded several shades further towards invisibility. Depression was my only identity, one that I wore like a cloak of shame.

My new guardian talked while I compulsively traced my finger along the seam of the chair's padded arm. The house rules were a more flexible version of those that I had endured at Sheldon. We were free to use the communal areas as needed. Any trips beyond the front door required the accompaniment of a staff member. Visitors were welcome every evening from 5:00 to 6:00 except Sunday. The staff referred to us as clients, not patients. We had rotating assignments for cooking dinner and washing dishes. A group session in cognitive behavior therapy and a meditation workshop were held each afternoon.

The main difference between Sheldon's and Beacon House's inventory of rules was a privilege that jolted me out of my slumped position. We could discharge ourselves from Beacon House anytime we wanted, with 24-hour notice. Our freedom wasn't dependent on the assessment of doctors or our ability to charm the attendants with feigned vitality. I signed the admittance paper and my keeper stood, picked up my paper luggage, and led me to my room.

I felt a fleeting moment of bliss when he pushed open the door to my new bedroom. The staff had meddled with the interior design over the course of years of creative curation. The results were an eccentric but endearing pallet of subdued colors and textures that made me want to close my eyes and sink into any one of the cushioned surfaces. The bed was covered with a thick quilted bedspread. An oversized easy chair was draped with a tartan afghan throw. There was a lamp so I could read before going to sleep and coat hangers in the closet so I could try to salvage my crumpled shirts. After the imposed austerity of the psychiatric ward I felt like I'd arrived at an opulent hotel.

When I lowered my head onto the pillow an hour later I clutched the blanket to my chin, anticipating the creeping dread that I knew would accompany me into agitated sleep. My subconscious was a masterful usher at escorting me to my front row seat in a theater of nightmares.

I awoke to the startling sight of daylight glinting along the edges of the window blinds. The digits of the electronic clock confirmed the legitimacy of the encroaching light. 7:00 AM had arrived. I had slept through the night without my usual bouts of insomnia.

The carpet felt stiff against the soles of my feet as I wandered into the hallway dressed in jeans and a t-shirt. Two new staff members—a middle age woman in a red sweater and a young man with his own carefully cultivated facial hair—looked up from their computer screens and greeted me as I entered the communal living space.

Three people were seated at the large dining table. I poured myself a cup of the weak coffee that seemed to be the universally mandated morning beverage for psychiatric facilities. I leaned against the formica countertop. The conversation had the halting rhythm of a group of people still struggling to become fully awake. Their sentences were punctuated by long silences and the creak of chairs as they shifted in their seats. I carried my cup to the end of the table and joined them. They greeted me with the perfunctory nods and brief eye contact of people accustomed to institutional environments and the revolving parade of new and departing faces.

Within minutes I knew how my stay in this house would unravel. The days would be monotonous. The group meetings would be dull. No aggressive attendants would rap loudly on our door at dawn or exhort us to attend meetings and workshops. We had all been referred here by doctors who recognized our growing ability to be independent. Every moment was a slow and steady countdown towards departure. Despite my glum resignation to the tedious days ahead, I knew that this stretch of time in a group residence was exactly what I needed after my headlong plunge into suicidal depression and the chaotic environment of a psychiatric hospital.

Nine days after the ambulance drivers unloaded me from the gurney in front of the watchful residents of Sheldon Psychiatric and four days after I entered Beacon House I returned to my home in Oakland. Daniel was my driver, picking me up at the appointed time in his car. With a few words and a wave goodbye to the staff of Beacon House my tour of Bay Area inpatient psychiatric facilities was complete.

The late summer weather was warm when we pulled into our driveway. Oak trees cast deep shade beneath the bright sun. Despite the bucolic setting I could feel myself sinking deeper into the passenger seat as Daniel brought the car to a stop. Our house seemed to suck all light and air out of its surroundings. The eaves, windows and door scowled beneath the blue skies. The brown exterior repelled light. I made a reluctant exit from the car and followed the walkway towards the front porch.

Halfway along this stone path I came to a halt. I didn't want to go forward, I didn't want to go backward, and I didn't want to remain where I was. I didn't want to die but I didn't want to live. It was an agonizing impasse. Suicidal depression's greatest conundrum isn't that we necessarily crave death, it's that we despise life. We want to live in a world where torment isn't integrated into the core of our being. We desire a metamorphosis that will transform us. Death isn't enticing us with its ethereal temptations, it is simply the only alternative available.

Daniel watched from the porch, his eyes blinking in rapidly growing alarm, until I finally forced myself to take a step forward, then another.

Major depression has the capacity to turn

reality into a garish funhouse of reflections. Every piece of furniture in the living room was laden with doom. The hallway from the kitchen to the bathroom was a corridor to suicide. The sunlight that beamed through the skylight etched glittering shards into the kitchen countertops.

Like any victim of a trauma, my return to the scene of the crime triggered powerful reactions. I set my paper bag on the kitchen counter with shaky hands, closed my eyes and forced myself to recall a platitude that had been recited to me like an incantation by patients, clinicians and staff. No emotion lasts forever, I said out loud. My voice sounded thin and high in the silence. It will shift, no matter how impossible that may seem, I continued. Daniel nodded in wide-eyed agreement. I didn't believe any of the words that I spoke, but they were the catalyst I needed to take another step deeper into the house.

Chapter 7

When a person leaves a hospital after being treated for a physical ailment that requires a finite period of convalescence—a fractured limb, say, or a routine surgery—they will, in a morally correct world, arrive home to find a gathering of family and friends awaiting their return. This small but intrepid group will pledge support toward the patient's recovery. Meals will be discussed, doctor appointments will be confirmed, pills will be divided into tidy plastic containers. Someone will initiate the email thread that will coordinate house visits, transportation and casserole delivery.

A person returning from a psychiatric hospital will likely arrive to a different kind of homecoming. A gathering of relatives, friends and neighbors will be conspicuously absent. This avoidance of personal interaction, initiated by the patient's spouse, is an attempt to alleviate discomfort for all parties. Potential caretakers will be excused from assisting a friend who suffers from a disease that challenges our familiarity with how to nurture sick people, and the arriving patient won't have to feign an ability to function in a world whose standard practices includes the routine expression of hope, optimism and happiness.

During the long string of days and nights that I'd lived with a shifting population of roommates a fantasy had periodically illuminated the tunnel vision that defined my world view. This imaginary scenario was inspired by a movie I'd encountered years before while scrolling through endless television entertainment options one evening. The film was a product of a past era, with the slow pacing and black and white cinematography that makes our modern attention spans crackle with impatience. A recurring setting appeared throughout the film. Scenes of a genteel mental sanatorium set in a country landscape invited movie-going audiences to witness the inspirational journey of the main character as he struggled with unforeseen mental burdens. This was an idealized version of a psychiatric facility. Patients strolled along stone paths or reclined on wicker furniture warmed by the sun. Their exact diagnosis is not stated, only inferred: melancholia, neurosis, phobias. Peaceful contemplation in a bucolic setting graced by attendants dressed in white uniforms is the proven cure.

I wanted my house to be that manicured Eden. I wanted to sit in a white chair on a rolling green lawn and be caressed by gentle breezes. To achieve this goal, I knew I had to implement drastic changes in our household.

Daniel is the gregarious social animal in our marriage and I am the deferential spouse who allows his partner wide latitude in planning social activities. His alarm and grief at my mental fragility made him an unexpected collaborator in our new household regimen. I imposed serenity with the grip of a benevolent despot. Daniel was no longer permitted noisy entrances through the front door on weekend afternoons with a group of our friends ready for margaritas on our back patio, or to entreat me to allow him to display a five-foot long stuffed tiger on the coffee table. We transformed a household that was spontaneous and unkempt into a disciplined and functional unit. June Cleaver would have been proud.

My aversion to returning to my job outweighed the risk of losing my position in the book publishing company where I worked. The rawness of my disease rendered me incapable of sitting through stultifying meetings in conference rooms or engaging in conversations with my colleagues that weren't sabotaged by my stammering voice. My psychiatrist and I both agreed that a one month respite from work was necessary and justified. My boss listened politely on the phone as I explained this prescribed thirty days of rest and then generously, and surprisingly, agreed to it.

When Daniel left the house each morning, offering me a daily dose of emotional support and his reiteration to call him immediately if I was feeling overwhelmed, I stared at the closing front door as if it were a vault clanging shut. I could recite the list of simple activities that he and I had created to keep me busy throughout the day: grocery shopping, dog walking, yard work, hiking, home projects, cooking, writing. Implementing them was another story.

I would wither beneath the perceived weight of these tasks. Encounters with the checkout clerk and other shoppers milling in line were loaded with harrowing variables. A drive on the freeway was a slow motion slide towards an invisible abyss. Neighbors trapped me with interminable stories. Dead bugs on the patio were victims of the suffering and impermanence that stalked all of us in the world. A microwaved chicken pot pie in front of the television was the path of least resistance. The couch became my refuge.

I had failed to mimic the arc of the lead character who enters the sanatorium a shambling wreck and departs a humble hero. On the day he leaves this institution he makes an emotional speech to the assembled nurses, doctors, staff and patients, expressing his gratitude. He cinches his suit pants high as he climbs into the car that will carry him to a rewarding new life.

My version of his triumphant journey was a stumbling disaster. I had tipped our home environment too far towards an extreme. Tormented thoughts will echo loudly in houses that are hushed and perfect. My despair had lost its shrillness but still retained its stifling presence.

Several weeks after my return home Daniel and I decided that we needed to break this spell of introversion. A major social event was approaching with the implacable forward motion of storm clouds on the horizon. Daniel and I had ignored its imminent arrival. Now we were both driven by an urgency to rejuvenate some of my atrophying social skills.

Our neighbor Erin was hosting her annual September BBQ. It was a large event, strategically planned for Northern California's warm autumn weather. Dozens of neighbors and friends from all parts of the Bay Area gathered for a long afternoon and evening of grilling smoky meats and drinking beer. Daniel and I had been loyal attendees for years. Our urge to attend this upcoming event was buoyed by the realization that the noise and interaction of a large outdoor party would be a form of immersive therapy for me.

We arrived late, delayed by my last-minute indecision on whether to wear a shirt that exhibited my enthusiasm for a festive gathering or one that reflected my somber state of mind. I settled on a short-sleeve button-down with a diamond pattern that seemed to convey both messages effectively. The few seconds that it took to ascend the five steps to Erin's backyard deck were sufficient for my trepidation to blossom into full blown anxiety. Guests filled the yard, forming daunting and impenetrable circles. Confident and interesting people were allowed access. Dreary arrivals were discouraged. I knew I had about five seconds before I would turn and flee so I pushed my way through the crowd towards the spot where Erin and a group of acquaintances were gathered.

She greeted me with a friendly hello and stepped aside to make space for me in the circle of guests. I fidgeted, wondering if a round of introductions was due, but the speed and volume of the conversation invalidated the need. A lively discussion was underway. Jokes darted back and forth.

The topic was marijuana and the conversation centered around an upcoming ballot measure that would allow the voters of Oakland to decide if the city should collect sales tax on medical marijuana. The opinions in favor of this bill clearly outweighed opposition to it. Wry commentary overrode serious observation. I listened, following the banter.

At first Erin's voice was just another sound in the chatter, and I failed to register its relevance. Then I realized that she was speaking to me. Her tone indicated that she was asking me a question.

Would I be able to afford the additional tax on my excessive pot habit? she asked. Her lip curled into a wry smile.

I felt my cheeks flush with heat. I don't smoke pot, I said. You know that, I told her. My voice was hard and chastising.

Her face flashed through a range of startled expressions. Rejection and confusion settled into a look of anger

Sorry, she said, turning sharply away.

I realized, with horror, that she had been joking. A month ago I would have recognized the social cues in her voice and would have joined in the joke, perhaps offering a caricature of a stoner blissfully perusing the snack section at a late-night convenience store. Now I felt nauseous.

The group was mired in silence. I could feel words trapped in the back of my throat. I wanted to explain my trauma, my plunge into depression, my disconnect from reality. I could show my contrition for this outburst. I could educate them.

Instead, I hurried away, sparing myself further humiliation. I cursed silently as I dodged the crowd. I'd made a terrible mistake. I should never have come to this social event. I was the unwelcome guest who leaves you hanging in awkward silence, the one you silently pray doesn't stand or sit next to you, the person who responds to a humorous anecdote with a sour rebuke. The world around me was untouched by the invisible rubble piled around me. I passed Daniel, his back turned as he told an anecdote to a captive audience, and grunted as I stepped down the stairs that led to open, unsullied air.

As I walked home I finally understood. Depression is a supremely adaptable disease. It thrives in chaos and it thrives in quiet. It is a vain narcissist and a dispassionate bystander. It is an impetuous opportunist and a cautious observer. It is as flexible as it is unyielding.

I managed to loosen this quagmire of toxic introspection enough to take a few measured breaths. Like the most truculent tyrants in our world, depression is also vulnerable. It needs our fear to feed its ravenous appetite. I had influence over this disease's ability to enervate, to deplete, to ruin. I had no idea how to implement this power but as I walked up the street, shaded by the trees that spread their limbs over this quiet stretch of asphalt, I let a glimmer of the possibility exist.

Chapter 8

Psychiatrists and mad scientists share one common passion: they are both fascinated with chemicals. The man in the rumpled white lab coat with the unkempt hair and thick eyeglasses loves to conduct his symphony of bubbling beakers. He squeezes several drops of clear solution into a shimmering vial then chortles as froth billows over the rim.

The tastefully dressed psychiatrist in black slacks and a cream-colored blouse speaks confidently from behind her desk as she informs her patient that the fourth medication she's prescribing has the potential to be the one that elevates him to a new level of mental health. Every mix of medications is a cocktail and every psychiatrist is the bartender.

Modern psychiatry has attempted to eliminate the archaic practices of past eras that resulted in a lifetime of institutionalization for the most debilitated victims of mental illness. Psychopharmaceuticals are now the first line of defense against major mental illness. These can be powerful anti-psychotics that will buckle the knees of the most agitated patient or antidepressants that gradually transform a person's thoughts over the course of weeks and months.

The tens of millions of pills that go out the doors of pharmacies across the United States are essential to the medical management of mental illness but they are only one piece of a larger system. Psychotherapy is the other major cog in this vast machine and words are the fuel that propel it. During a fifty-minute session of talk therapy an MSW, MFT, LCSW or other credentialed professional will use their experience and training to try and counter the bleak perspective of a client living with major depression. They will tell us we are not alone and that millions of people affected by depression have learned to live fulfilling and positive lives. They'll tell us that we may feel hopeless now but we will rediscover a sense of purpose and meaning.

During the first months after leaving the hospital I was immune to these empty phrases. I ignored them as they echoed off the walls of the meeting rooms and offices where I participated in sessions, consultations and group therapy.

My skepticism was based on a fundamental aspect of the psychotherapy process. These mental health specialists are trained to remain professionally detached. The dynamic of a client-therapist relationship is firmly weighted in one direction. The client divulges, and the therapist doesn't. Their personal struggles, behaviors, traits, substance abuse issues, food preferences and sex lives remain solidly and privately located on their side of the room. They are our observers, not our peers.

The best advice I received for surviving suicidal depression came from the experts: those survivors of pills and razor blades, of belts cinched around the neck, of watery plunges. They told me that the grip of an overdose as it drags you to the bottom of consciousness gives you just enough time to regret your decision. You can attempt to bargain with or rebel against the forces that are carrying you beyond the point of no return but those forces alone have the power to grant or deny your pleas.

I felt connected to these fellow travelers. I had visited similar terrain. They offered insight culled from experience: the vast majority of people who experience severe depression aren't resigned to it, they are trying to manage it; the disease doesn't discriminate based on race, gender, ethnicity, sexual orientation, religion or economic background; we don't want to be sick with this disease, the disease wants us to be sick; major depressive disorder may never be dispelled, or crushed, or cured, but it can be managed; the large majority of suicide is committed in moments of impulse.

This last comment was the one that electrified my neural pathways. The urge to die can have an immediacy that is breathtaking. Then, in a turnaround that defies our grimmest expectations, it can fade or pass, within minutes, hours or days, leaving us both relieved and nervously anticipating the next round of deadly urges that may besiege us.

When lethal ruminations haunt us they can stick with a tenacity that is nearly debilitating. During these treacherous periods of time I try and remember the voices of the survivors. They tell us that there is always an alternative to suicide. If our disconnect from hope and survival becomes so absolute that we elevate our destruction above all other alternatives we must implement life-saving techniques. A suicidal plan is just as dangerous as a hemorrhaging wound and needs the same critical attention. A call to 911 takes only seconds, a drive to the emergency room takes minutes. Initiating these actions can fill us with an immobilizing shame or a stinging dread of the grim atmosphere of hospitals and wards but there is a more convincing argument for taking these steps: they are a short-term investment in a long-term future. None of these trips to institutions are permanent. With every major depressive episode or plunge into despondency that we survive we gain a better understanding of this disease. Perspective becomes our foundation for survival. This is a philosophy espoused by the survivors who encountered their own stark epiphany at the last possible moment and became advocates for life instead of death.

Chapter 9

With each successive birthday that we celebrate as we approach the middle years of our lives, smiling politely as a chorus of well-wishers belt out a grating rendition of the birthday song, there is an intangible shiver in our conscience. For one unsettling moment we're reminded that we've moved one year closer to the end of our time on this planet and one year further from our arrival into it. We aim our lips at the candles on the cake and dispel this disturbing thought along with the blast of air that quells the flames.

We believe that we've successfully expelled this unwelcome antagonist from our subconscious until one afternoon, weeks or months later, when it pops back to the surface, sending ripples across our consciousness as we grip the pole on a swaying subway train or drive a car full of teenagers to a soccer game or manicure the topiary animals in our front yard. The sting that it conveys is an existential thorn in our side. The past grows, the future shrinks, and death is no longer an irrelevant blip on the outer edge of our radar.

In our younger years these blips are faint transmissions from a distant galaxy. We are indestructible. Our subconscious is still a spacious vessel. We haven't yet had to juggle the kinetic elements of money, work, relationships, family and emotions in a marathon feat of sweaty agility. Dropping any one of them can bring a thudding halt to all of them.

Gurus, philosophers, hitchhikers, lifestyle coaches, bartenders and all the other citizens of the world who have ever practiced the art of introspection or stared too long at the bottom of an empty beer glass have abundant wisdom to dispense. One day at a time, practice what you preach, buy low sell high, location location location, say your prayers and, at the top of the heap, the fastest route to personal fulfillment: live in the moment. Every day we remind ourselves to apply this concept to our lives, and every day we falter. Paychecks shrink, children rebel, relationships sour, emotions erupt, discord simmers and we find ourselves fixated on the future or dwelling on the past rather than allowing the world around us to unfold in real time.

I understand the sharp tug that memories can exert on us at any unexpected moment. We imbue the past with hues applied from an elaborate palette. In my previous life, before the breakdown that etched its mark into the chronology of life, my senses were fully engaged, complex and rewarding. Colors were rich, food was sublime, emotions were immersive, intimacy was sensual.

On the evening that I left the psychiatric hospital, walking side by side across the parking lot with the young volunteer who accompanied me to her car on that summer night, I realized that these experiences were lost to me. I looked around me as we crossed the asphalt and I felt like I was a stranger in a foreign land. I was numb to the trees gently rustling in the breeze, the streetlights casting a luminous glow on the roofs and hoods of cars, the warmth of the night air, the casual chattiness of my companion. Reference points were lost. I had become immune to the world that pulsed around me.

Now I visit my memories like a tourist who has wandered into an art museum after closing time. The enormous canvasses and sculptures are muted by the reduced light. I lean towards the surfaces of these pieces, trying to discern colors. Sometimes there will be glimmers of red, green or gold hidden in a crevasse. Usually the paintings repel scrutiny. I peer at them, aware of the artistry but detached from their beauty.

Chapter 10

Church comes in a hundred different forms. A steeple and a town square, a cathedral and a priest, retreats, labyrinths, a rabbi and a synagogue, a mosque and an imam, temples, shrines, group therapy and twelve-step programs.

My new church was a large rectangular room with beige walls and two tall windows at one end. It was located in the psychiatric department that I visited almost daily in Oakland over the course of a three-week period.

A half dozen plain brown conference tables were pushed together in the middle of the room to form a rectangular hub. Approximately twenty-five people would gather around these tables at 9:00 AM each day and settle into the rows of chairs that ringed them. Some of us arrived alert and energetic, initiating conversations with early morning zeal. Some shuffled through the door with a yawn of sleepiness or boredom barely suppressed.

The meeting started when a group of four or five men and women entered the room together. Those of us in attendance turned to watch this small procession. Although the arriving group was unadorned by any official emblem of authority, their clipboards, pens, file folders and jangling keys indicated their status. They filled the row of empty chairs at the head table and spread papers across the horizontal surface. These were the psychiatrists and therapists who would guide us through the next four hours of the day. Once they were seated one of them would stand, greet the gathered group and the meeting would commence.

This program was called Intensive Outpatient Therapy. It was designed for people in mental crisis. Everyone present, except for the program leaders, had either just emerged from a dire episode of hospitalization or were precariously poised at the cusp of one. Four mornings a week, we arrived at this communal space and began a daily routine.

The session started with introductions. Each participant would stand, say their first name and state a goal they hoped to achieve that day. The list of proposed accomplishments revealed the fragility of our aspirations. Take out the trash, refill depleted medications, reduce an afternoon nap from two hours to one, arrive at work on time, change the cat's litter box—these were some of the typical objectives. Ambition had long been modified in favor of prosaic pursuits.

The ostensible reason for these introductions was to create rapport among strangers and to inspire each speaker with a sense of purpose. The underlying motive was more strategic. As each of us stood for our brief announcement in front of the group, two of the therapists jotted notes. Our moods, goals and comments were being recorded. A selection process was underway.

The panel seated at the head of the table guided us through the first hour of the morning. We had meditation sessions, written exercises in cognitive behavior therapy and stretching exercises that gently splayed our bodies on the carpeted floor. It was our spiritual, physical and psychological breakfast.

When the wall clock's minute hand had completed a full revolution around the dial the facilitators would make a few final scribbles on their clipboards, rustle their papers and announce the end of the meeting. As we filtered out the door, they reminded us to return in twenty minutes for the next segment of the day's program.

We left the room in the orderly formation of adults being excused to recess. The small band of cigarette smokers immediately adjourned to the sidewalk adjacent to the clinic. The majority of us gravitated to a large outdoor courtyard where landscaped gardens mingled with wooden benches and we could occupy our time with strolls along gravel paths. Those of us that remained inside the building loitered in the hallway. We glanced periodically at a single office door until we heard the click of its latch. The door would swing open and one of the therapists would step into the hallway and pin a sheet of paper to a small cork board on the wall, then disappear back into the room, a jack in the box returning to her lair.

This was our cue to gather in front of the newly posted document, like a gaggle of high school theater students eagerly reading the casting results for the next school play.

The names of all the IOP participants had been divided into four groups. We were assigned to spend the next 90 minutes with an intimate gathering of five or six of our companions who were experiencing similar mental struggles to ours. The notes that had been jotted earlier in the morning by the staff, capturing our perceived moods, now united us. Phase two of our day had begun.

These smaller group therapy sessions took place in rooms located throughout the building. A cluster of chairs would be gathered in the center of the room, with a floor lamp in the corner casting an ambient glow. A therapist would seat herself in the circle, an egalitarian location among the participants around her.

Anna was one of the first people who gained my attention during group meetings in IOP. When she shared with the group it was clear she was a veteran of this disease. She knew the lexicon fluently. Healthy habits for a good night's sleep were called sleep hygiene. Gradually increasing the dosage of a new medication was titration. Psychiatrists were referred to as Pdocs. She was an alcoholic in recovery for over fifteen years, an integral part of her identity that she mentioned every time it was her turn to share with those of us gathered around her. She had hair the color of a raging wildfire and a single silver stud piercing her left nostril. She favored black outfits from head to toe, the fashion of a woman who shunned the sun.

The first time I heard her speak, distilling decades of her life into a few potent drops, I roused myself from my brooding introspection and listened. Her depression had started when she was a teenager. There had been peaks and valleys, an intentional overdose and years of trial and error with different antidepressants and adjunct medications. She'd experienced long stretches of stability and inverse periods struggling to survive the suffocating dual grip of despair and despondency. I was still lurching my way through each hour of our daily classes. She was a role model for a newly diagnosed patient learning how to manage a disease that picks off its victims at a slow but steady rate.

My fellow IOP members tossed around phrases and acronyms that made me feel like a sixth grader tagging along with a gang of swaggering older students. MDD, GAD, MDE, BP, OCD, SSRI and PD were some of the clusters of consonants that rolled off their tongues. Eventually I would learn their meanings but in those early days there was no abbreviation or language that could translate the dimensions of my despair into recognizable terms. I adopted the single word "fine" as a defense against any intrusions into my state of mind.

One morning as the discussion bounced back and forth between group members my thoughts were interrupted by a few key words. I heard the name Sylvia Plath spoken by Anna in her husky voice. She was saying that Plath had created the perfect metaphor for depression. An image of the cover of the book The Bell Jar popped into my mind, dredged from a memory born almost forty years earlier. It was a paperback, laden with heavy black type intertwined with a wilted rose. Plath's most famous book was a sharp testament to youthful disillusionment and a frank exploration of mental illness. During my teenage years as one of a small army of soulful, artistic high school students the book had catalyzed the emotions that I craved so strongly in those days. Sorrow, happiness, fear, desire and joy made my youthful brain tremble with passion.

In that IOP meeting in Oakland, surrounded by people whose ideals had all been trampled by the weight of depression, I realized that Plath was making her second major impact on my life. The bell jar that she depicted epitomized my experience. I was the inhabitant of a sealed world, deprived of hope. Anna had unintentionally resurrected a dormant memory and imbued it with a new meaning.

Sasha was another fellow traveler through the Intensive Outpatient Program. If Anna was the wan presence in the group, Sasha was her opposite. Her skin was ebony and her hair was a short, stylish bob. She was filled with fitful energy that kept her fingers constantly in motion on the arm of her chair or top of her knee. Sasha wore slacks, tailored jackets and high heels unblemished by scuff marks.

Sasha was scheduled to be married in one month. Over 150 invited guests from the Bay Area and across the United States had purchased plane tickets, reserved cars and booked hotel rooms nearby. Bouquets of white roses had been ordered that would flank the church pulpit during the ceremony. A banquet hall had been rented and a catering company had been retained with a deposit large enough to fund a trip to a luxury tropical resort.

Panic constricted Sasha's eyes as she told us about the grotesque rebellion that her body had launched. Trembling hands and a perpetually dry mouth were the milder inconveniences. The most debilitating symptom was her inability to sleep. Her life resembled the steady trudge of a wide-eyed sleepwalker through each day. During the darkest hours of the night, when our eyelids should be performing their fluttering ode to R.E.M. sleep, Sasha's mind would launch into dizzying flight. Anxiety that pounces at 3:00 AM has a stark advantage over its prey. Our defenses are disengaged, lulled by twilight consciousness and the absence of the stimulation that keeps millions of synapses firing during waking hours. We have no buffer against night phantasms that loom over our bed like ghoulish visitors.

Large weddings are a form of civilized torture. The infinite details that must be managed, from the opacity of the vellum insert in the invitations to choosing vegan and gluten-free menu options, are tasks for only the most indomitable type A personality. This was perhaps Sasha's biggest source of despair. She was a prime candidate to manage her own wedding, a professional businesswoman who could keep the department at her workplace both productive as well as respectful of her equanimity, yet she was failing spectacularly at the biggest event of her life.

Surprisingly, she had no anxiety about her commitment to her future husband, and no doubts about his commitment to her. This awareness offered little reprieve from her realization that something as simple as two people planning a future together could throw her mental equilibrium into chaos.

Her visit to the psychiatry department had resulted in a prescription for a sedative and an antidepressant as well as a referral to the IOP program. Listening to Sasha talk, her voice racing skittishly ahead of her thoughts, I realized the gravity of her situation. Anxiety loves a deadline. It rehearses obsessively for the moment when it will sabotage a celebration by reducing its host to a panicked, incoherent public wreck.

Sasha was at least twenty years younger than me, and a woman, and black, yet I felt a strong affinity with her. She too was trying to recover from an acute crisis that she didn't understand and couldn't control.

During my first few days in these small groups I avoided eye contact with my companions and our moderator, preferring a fixed view of the carpet to the confessions and opinions of people under the influence of their own volatile moods. The Intensive Outpatient Program was aptly named. I had expected these sessions to echo the style of the meetings and workshops I'd attended in the psychiatric hospital and transitional housing. Those gatherings were erratic and unpredictable, starting late and finishing early, frequently interrupted by outbursts from nearby residents who decided to add their own opinions to the discussion. The IOP meetings operated within the constraints of professional etiquette. The voluntary attendance of each individual and their awareness that they were foundering at the edge of dire mental instability created group sessions that were charged by a dynamic current.

My reason for avoiding participation was altruistic. In my solipsistic version of reality I harbored a secret that I knew was too deadly to share. The people that surrounded me had suffered psychic lacerations, mental breakdowns and suicide attempts. They were susceptible to even the mildest outside influences. I would have been a traitor by exposing them to my virulent thoughts.

On my fourth day in IOP I could feel the gaze of the therapist lingering on me for a protracted period of time. The countdown to my participation was accelerating. Before she could extend her usual invitation for me to speak I opened my mouth and started talking. I tried to restrain the words that tumbled out of me but they gained their own momentum. My secret was both sincere and disgraceful: I was obsessed with suicide. In the grocery store, as I emptied my cart at the checkout aisle I envisioned myself in a car swirling with invisible billows of carbon monoxide. While talking to Daniel at dinner with a forkful of green beans poised near my lips I was staring over the railing of the Golden Gate Bridge at frothy whitecaps hundreds of feet below. When I brushed my teeth I imagined the sleek pressure of a razor's edge pressed into my wrist. I confessed my shame that I felt like a fraud and a coward, too afraid to follow through with these fervent desires, yet fearful that someday I might.

No one in the circle spoke. I cringed, realizing that this traumatized group of human beings was either cowering at the aggression of my actions or fuming at my callousness. All around me, my colleagues advocated for surviving depression. I dreamed of dying from it.

Then came a chorus of voices. I scrambled to decipher them. My companions were reassuring me that I wasn't alone. They had experienced the same unrelenting cycles of suicidal despair in the past, or were currently struggling with them, or had heeded the destructive commands of those insistent voices. Our therapist overrode the noise with a booming request for quiet. She told me that suicidal ideation was understandable in the aftermath of a major depressive episode. She reiterated that a fascination with death without the compulsion to act on it is a cause for concern but not for intervention. A shaky sense of relief settled through me. Suicide was the skeleton in our collective closet. Opening the doors to these concealed chambers lessened the stigma of their contents. I leaned forward, drawing closer to the center of the group. I wanted to hug everyone gathered in a circle around me and thank them for sharing my dirty secret.

Chapter 11

Antidepressants are stealthy drugs. They tunnel their way into the fortress of a depressed mind, burrowing under the dank moat and turreted walls, making steady progress towards the center of this insular domain. Despite stalwart resistance from their host, they disperse throughout their new environment. Once they have established a foothold these agitators coerce the neurotransmitters serotonin, norepinephrine and other chemical messengers to step up their contribution to the bustling biological network that they inhabit.

Antidepressants enter our consciousness long before we pop the first of these pink, yellow, white or blue pills into our mouths. They are part of our cultural backdrop from the moment we are mature enough to absorb the barrage of advertising campaigns designed to induct fledgling consumers into the magnetic promises of products, values, commodities, ideologies and identities.

Media campaigns for antidepressants have a major advantage over almost every other product that sings, dances or struts its way across the screen. These drugs offer a payoff that is almost illusory in its promise. The concept of happiness has always been merchandised to the point of excess, from the close-up shots of tantalizing fast food to sleek gleaming cars gliding along winding country roads to burnished visions of eternal youth and beauty. Pharmaceutical companies are in the unique position of being able to nudge this promise an exponential leap higher. They offer a version of happiness that is permanent and enduring, the kind that doesn't disappear after the last juicy bite has been swallowed or the engine of our precision driving machine goes silent or we apply another layer of moisturizer to the skin around our eyes. Feelings of unworthiness will be replaced by feelings of fulfillment and contentment. We will finally arrive at the future we've been chasing.

When antidepressants gained their earliest prominence in the medical establishment they were heralded as a potentially revolutionary treatment. They were a pathway to relief for people riven with internal strife. Psychiatrists engaged in consultations with their patients before determining the best course of treatment.

Now, virtually every doctor, from general internists to specialized practitioners, writes prescriptions for antidepressants, frequently after the most perfunctory discussions with a patient. The breakneck evolution of technology and media has created an environment where professional evaluation and advertising are almost inseparable. Doctors used to prescribe prescription drugs, but now the pharmaceutical companies have joined the medical team.

I resented every single pill that I threw back with a gulp of water in the first year after my release from the hospital. I berated myself for falling into dependency on drugs. Despite these self-recriminations I took my medication with steadfast respect for timing and schedule, laying the pills on the bathroom counter each morning and night without variation. I wanted to feel better. I wanted to defeat this disease.

Some people call them happy pills, but those aren't the people that actually take them. Happy pills are the ones that you buy in an exchange of twenty dollar bills in a parking lot and then, after they've coursed through your bloodstream, propel you into a dance club, concert hall or house party for an evening of gyrating to music along with a crowd of other sweaty pleasure seekers.

Antidepressants are their distant, stodgy relatives. They make you work for your happiness. They keep your head above choppy waters while you watch the party boat float by. They show you the light at the end of the tunnel but never shine it on you. They are purchased under the scrutiny of sensible pharmacists in brightly lit environments where you wait patiently in line for your turn at the counter. As an added sting, these medications frequently inflict distress on their consumers. The list of side effects is a minefield of contradictions: diarrhea or constipation, anxiety or apathy, loss of appetite or overeating, insomnia or somnolence, libido diminishment or increased arousal.

Months into my first combination of medications I realized that something had shifted in my outlook. My infatuation with death no longer occupied every moment of my waking life. I wasn't cured. I still ruminated on dying. But I didn't do it all the time, driven by the voracious appetite of a starving man. The antidepressants had prevailed at destabilizing their onerous target.

Studies of major depression confirm the slippery grip of suicidal urges. The majority of suicides and attempted suicides are impulsive. The

131

decision to die occurs within one hour of the actual act for up to 80% of suicidal people. Five minutes, or one hour, or a succession of days are interminable periods of time when our internal compass points rigidly towards the termination of our own life. We are positive that our mental despair is permanent, chronic, irreversible. Our nearly impossible task is to tell ourselves that this state of despondency will shift, will change, will transform.

Impulsive acts are the result of sudden, strong and unreflective urges. This precise definition limits the extent of their influence over us. With each successful passage we make through a gauntlet of suicidal urges our experience becomes a tool for survival. Each day that we are alive puts us one step closer to understanding a system that is damaged and bent but not irrevocably broken.

Chapter 12

Pharoahs reigned and died, Rome rose and fell, Sony Walkmen came and went, but depression has been afflicting the occupants of this planet for thousands of years without pause. The ancient Greeks called it the disease of melancholia, a condition characterized by "all fears and despondencies." Modern science has both expanded and distilled the definition of this disease over the past century. Depression is too enigmatic to be clearly understood, too familiar to be unknown and too publicized to be ignored.

During an appointment with one of the many therapists I spoke to during my hospitalization and its immediate aftermath I jabbed my forefinger in the air and announced that I hated this disease. She corrected me. "It's classified as a disorder," she said, "not a disease." I asked her to clarify the difference. "Medical lexicon," she answered. In other words, none.

Disease is the right word for my condition. When depression is in its most pernicious state, it feels like cancer. Something raw and malignant is gnawing at my brain, like a demented squirrel working its way towards the core of an unshelled nut.

On expensive couches in private offices and in stiff plastic chairs in generic waiting rooms psychologists and psychiatrists will lean forward and provide a patient, still reeling from the impact of a major depressive episode, and their family, anxious to understand the fearful changes affecting their loved one, with a framework to identify this bewildering collection of mental and physical ailments. Mental health professionals have adopted an analogy that I heard innumerable times during my progression through facilities, therapy sessions and group meetings. They compare major depressive disorder to diabetes. Both diseases are chronic and both require daily medication. Both have a high profile in Western epidemiology. Like depression, diabetes has been inflicting mortality on humans for thousands of years. Experts use the two "D" words side by side to emphasize the fact that both these diseases need to be carefully managed.

These two diseases are similar in their chronic

nature but separated by major gaps in the efficacy of treatment. Diabetes has benefited from rapid progress in research and implementation. Survival rates continue to improve. This illness has been successfully illuminated by a probing medical spotlight.

Depression is still a shadowy perpetrator. The ability of antidepressants to alleviate major depression is controversial, garnering both criticism and support, from the far end of the spectrum where conspiracy theorists regard them as a stealthy plot by big pharmaceutical companies to rake in billions of dollars, to the accomplished researchers who affirm their ability to combat self-destructive thinking and save lives.

After my return home I fell into the compulsive habit of chasing this specter across the Internet with thousands of clicks and keystrokes. The sheer volume of opinions, anecdotes, discourse and speeches triggered unsettling feelings of animosity in me. Cyberspace seemed to be occupied by an army of depressed people intent on leaving their mark in every corner of the digital realm. I was suspicious of their motives. They were making excuses for indulgent behavior. They didn't suffer from a disease, they had embraced a fad. Depression was just another trend in privileged nations where too much leisure time led to too much self-absorption. The more I felt the rancor rising in me the more my criticism jelled.

The source of my antipathy towards these people so eager to promote their cause quickly became uncomfortably clear to me. I was a depressionphobe. The explosive growth of this ailment in modern society had triggered an unbalanced disdain that festered in me.

Like many phobic people, I was afflicted with the very thing that offended me in others. I became an equal opportunity bigot, directing my vitriol inward as well as outward. The only legitimately depressed people are those that kill themselves, or make a sincere effort to do so. Everyone else is an impostor. Not only did depression make me feel like a failure in my life and my relationships, it made me feel like a failure in depression.

I also expended an unwarranted amount of mental energy imagining the judgement of my friends. When they were in my presence they were attentive and sympathetic. The moment they gathered for a drink in a bar or sat down to dinner their attitude changed. My condition dominated their conversations. Was I depressed or just sad? Did I fixate on painful thoughts? Was I seeking attention? Did I need spiritual intervention? Did I drink too much? Did I get enough exercise? Our tendency as humans to analyze the behavior of the sick person, a known entity, rather than the disease, a biological riddle, is frequently the preferred path to determining the source of the suffering.

Depression is a disease of introversion. I had turned myself nearly inside out from staring at my battered psyche. The members of our therapy groups would share soul-numbing stories about dismal weekends hiding from friends or, as a novelty, rosy stories of productive days and contented nights. I would watch their mouths open and close in a cartoonish sync with the dialogue playing in my head. The words that I recited, like a silent mantra, ran in a churlish loop. I was contemptible. I had failed to practice the right combination of relaxation, invigoration, engagement, communication, diet, perfection, friendship, intimacy, kindness, love. I was a failure at every level.

All of us living with major depressive disorder need to tell ourselves—and struggle deeply to do so—that we have a disease equal to any other chronic disease out there in the world. It can vary in intensity, manifestation and symptoms. There can be flare-ups and remissions. We can't cure it by smiling more, the unsolicited advice offered by strangers or well-intentioned friends. We need to take our medications, engage in social activities, value our health and attempt to provide ourselves with as much self-love, forgiveness and strength as we can muster on the bad days and the good. It is hard work, but the payoff—those periods of time, both extended and brief, when hope soothes us with its remarkable presence—makes it worthwhile.

Chapter 13

The downside of a major depressive episode is that you are confined to a locked psychiatric ward. The stainless steel doors that swing inward so effortlessly when you are admitted to the hospital aren't as accommodating in the opposite direction. The doorway is flanked twenty four hours a day by an admittance desk on one side and a security guard in a blue uniform on the other. Even if a patient possessed with the misguided aspiration of achieving freedom made a mad dash through the doors, they would have to dodge the row of chairs in the visitor waiting room, race past the receptionist desk, then sprint across a large, flat parking lot. A single gazelle on an open plain would be less of an easy target for interception.

The upside is that you don't have to go to work every day. The fantasies of freedom that taunt our fatigued minds in the middle of a long afternoon on the job are no longer futile reverie.

Suddenly, and with blunt deliverance, we are free of moody bosses and the repetition of telephones, meetings, customers, technology, machinery, clients, quotas, deadlines, expectations. This new freedom extends into all the rote aspects of domestic life. We are no longer responsible for preparing meals, washing laundry, being polite to visiting houseguests or scooping food into a bowl for obstreperous children or impatient pets. A locked psychiatric ward is a vacation in its most dystopian form.

Then comes the day we are released. Papers have been signed, our spouse or friend waits patiently at our side, the nurse behind the desk watches while we grapple with a paper bag full of clothes, the security guard steps aside and we cross the threshold into freedom.

For a person struggling with mental illness, the transition from confinement to independence can be a smorgasbord of treacherous choices. We're emerging from a regimented life that includes monitored medication, a daily schedule and the routine assessment of professional healthcare providers. Now we must rely on our own discipline and motivation to guide ourselves through each day.

When we flip open our calendar it is a series

of blinding white pages. The insistent voices of my fellow psychiatric residents and the stern commands of Dr. Aldred crowded my brain, assailing me like a Greek chorus. Be social. Stay busy. Don't isolate. Fill the pages with activities, plans, dates, places, things.

People seek the company of other people because they want to be engaged. This sounds like the dream goal of every man and woman attending a speed dating event on a Friday night, scurrying from table to table with their glass of white wine in hand. Mental health professionals also have a love affair with this word, but they have anointed it with a less romantic meaning. Engagement is a survival technique. When our faltering mental health locks our gaze inward we are frequently staring at a landscape that would have made Hieronymus Bosch jealous. There is acrid smoke or vast voids of open space. There is environmental disaster, sexual violence, school shootings, terrorist attacks, civil war, virulent homophobia, institutionalized racism, rampant misogyny and poverty all crammed together in one infernal tableau.

Engagement is a paltry splash of water on this fiery inferno, but even a small dose can bring relief. Our five senses are lifelines to an outer world. The most mundane conversation with the grocery clerk, no matter how much it makes us fidget in discomfort, can disrupt our self-absorption for a few crucial minutes. The slow-motion poetry of a tai chi class that we witness in a park can lift our spirits just long enough to allow us to momentarily forget that our planet is doomed and living is pointless. My husband offering me a peanut butter sandwich in the middle of the afternoon can temporarily distract me from the chill of my introversion.

Engagement doesn't end with our own species. The man in San Francisco who, in a piece of disruptive public theatre protesting legalized gay marriage publicly demanded the right to marry his dog (who was too smart to bark his consent), may have been more of a psychologist than he knew. The limpid eyes and wet-nosed nuzzle of a beloved pet have the power to bring respite from mental pain.

Humans and pets are sensible allies in our mission to lighten the weight of overwhelming hopelessness but they come with limitations. I decided, after returning to the real world from the unorthodox one I had occupied for so many days, to refrain from sharing my most disturbing thoughts with my friends. My conscience was a vigilant referee. Whenever I wandered into territory that touched upon the vision of destitution I saw for myself and all people an internal alarm would remind me to stop.

Psychotherapists are built to endure the kind of grim narrative that we spare our friends and relatives. Death wishes, delusional thinking, violent fantasies and other torrid disturbances of the mind are just some of the forms of despair they encounter during an average work week. The education and training that culminated in the framed license hanging on their wall has hopefully prepared them for our onslaught of emotional pain.

A first session with a therapist can evoke the same mix of anticipation and trepidation as an impending blind date. Our fear that we will reveal the depravity of our ugliest thoughts mingles with the tantalizing prospect that this stranger will be the one that saves us from the existential ache that greets us in the morning and lulls us to sleep at night.

Several months after my release from the psychiatric hospital I drove to my first meeting with my new therapist. Violet Manning's office was located in her home in the Outer Richmond district of San Francisco, a neighborhood that sprawled along the western edge of the city and terminated in blustery Ocean Beach. These endless city blocks give credence to the famous quote, inaccurately attributed to Mark Twain, that "the worst winter I ever spent was a summer in San Francisco." No resident moves into this western part of the city unaware of its reputation for being blanketed in fog for months at a time.

I sat on the edge of the beige loveseat in her office and silently vowed to resist all attempts to penetrate my guarded emotions. For months my mind had been a pincushion for a slew of probing questions about my mental health. My body had been the test lab for a glut of psycho-pharmaceuticals. Here in this room, with my new therapist seated six feet from me in her comfortably worn leather chair, I forced myself to exude stability.

Violet jotted notes on a legal pad as I responded to her questions with calm renditions of my hospitalization, my panic attacks, my medications, my recent round of IOP, my depression.

How was my job going? she asked.

Smoothly, I told her, deferring any information about the dread that knotted my stomach each morning as I walked through the door to my workplace.

How have you been sleeping?

Pretty well, I told her, suppressing the urge to reveal that shadowy figures swarmed around my head each night, invoking insomnia.

How have your moods been? she asked.

I wanted to cackle like a wicked Halloween witch. The transitions from despondency to hope to futility to contentment to despair gave me emotional whiplash all day long.

Pretty steady, I told her.

Violet let the room go silent while her right foot did a slow motion tap dance on the floor. I shifted my gaze to the space on the wall behind her head and waited.

We were both veterans of this process. I had been seeing therapists throughout Northern California for much of my adulthood, starting with a visit to a college counselor during my freshman year. There was nothing unfamiliar about this current session with Violet. The technique of letting the client sit in silence was a common one for encouraging mired feelings to loosen.

For the remaining thirty minutes I surprised myself with my resilience. She tried to lure my emotions out of me. I responded with slippery rebukes. My answers weren't intended as skirmishes. This was a place where an exchange between a therapist and a client permits behavior both good and bad, active and detached, effusive and reserved. I was sick and tired of hearing myself and others talk, analyze, speculate, deduce.

I nodded when Violet finally announced that our time was up. She reminded me that she would see me next week. I handed her the check for $125 that culminated our session.

I felt invigorated as I drove my car out of the fog bank and into the sunshine that favored the rest of the city. Golden Gate Park was lush, the ornamental conceit of San Francisco's elaborate Victorian homes was endearing, the aggressive drivers in the urban traffic engaged me in a competitive game I enjoyed.

Forty minutes later, I stood in front of the refrigerator in my house, peering into the bright interior. My sense of satisfaction had transformed into an urge for an afternoon snack.

I pulled a package from the chilly interior then another from an adjacent cupboard and placed them on the granite countertop. The baby carrots had a sharp, sweet crunch. A few roasted almonds added a nutty flavor. I chewed serenely until the moment that I tried to swallow.

Instead of joining the collective effort, my

throat refused to cooperate. I could feel the panicky reaction when food hits the wrong mark and the gag reflex is triggered. I managed, with effort, to force a small portion past the point of the resistance, and then another.

This rejection was accompanied by other physical reactions. Sweat trickled from my armpits and seeped into my shirt. My hands trembled as I reached to put the lid on the can of almonds.

My repressed emotions were rattling the bars of the Freudian jail I had built. Like any prisoners denied access to the elements of life that are essential to survival - food, water, shelter, hope - they will agitate to have their voices heard. This revolt can last for minutes, hours, days or, in extreme circumstances, a lifetime. We may try to drive them back into their cells but the backlash can be brutal.

Fortunately, I was beginning to understand the interlocking pieces that hold my mental health together. Every person is the crossing guard for their emotions. We wait on the corner with our bright red stop sign in hand. We need to allow our disobedient, disruptive feelings equal access to the same crosswalk where our well-behaved little darlings also walk. Each of these knotty bundles of desires and demands needs to complete their journey to the other side of the street.

Chapter 14

Car owners and pill poppers have a lot in common. Some of us have never looked under the hood of our Mercedes S550 sports coupe or Kia minivan and never will. We reach out to flip the lever that releases the latch to this fearsome tangle of machinery and our hand recoils. Even the most timid of glances into the engine compartment might reveal a bolt dangling from a main sprocket or a ragged clump of fur stuck to a fan blade. We're happy to let professional mechanics take the risks associated with these murky crevasses.

Some of us approach our medications with the same attitude. We limit our curiosity to the single line of bold text printed on our prescription bottle. These instructions tell us how many pills to take and when to take them. All the other information written on the bottle invites trouble. We trust our doctors and have no wish to imperil that faith.

There is a group of medicated consumers who

choose an opposite approach. We become too fascinated with our pills. We read every word stamped on the label, peering at the microscopic text tucked along the bottom edge. We're convinced that we're being shrewd detectives, not hypochondriacs, as we decode the generic name, the brand name, the expiration date, the manufacturer, the RX number and all other printed minutiae.

Several days after returning home from my stays in Sheldon Psychiatric and Beacon House I made a trip to the pharmacy. As I navigated through the streets of Oakland I felt the pleasure of being behind the wheel of a car after almost two weeks deprived of that experience

I explained to the woman behind the pharmacy counter that I was picking up a refill. She ran her fingers over the keys on her computer then informed me that my prescription would be ready in ten minutes. A glance at the rows of people seated in waiting room chairs indicated the inflated optimism of her estimate.

I lowered myself into chair and started performing online searches on my phone. Every prescription drug was a new frontier in those early days. I wanted to learn more about this medication stored somewhere in one of the tall white cabinets behind the pharmacy counter, waiting to be measured into a pill bottle marked with my name.

Within minutes I was immersed in an Internet forum the length of a Russian novel. The contributors to this particular online venue offered opinions that ranged from adulation to condemnation. It wasn't the raw emotion of these posts that made me blanch with distress. It was the sheer volume of medications these writers were consuming. Antidepressants, antipsychotics, mood stabilizers, sedatives and stimulants were the steady diet of most of these authors. Three medications a day seemed to be the norm. Four was common. Many were taking enough pills to make the infamous Broadway actress Neely O'Hara look like a venerated health guru.

I lowered my phone, closed my eyes, and tried to let the tension dissipate. These online writers had voluntarily wandered down the path of dependency. I vowed not to become the patient whose visit to the pharmacy culminates in a bag of booty as weighty as a fifth grader's sack of Halloween candy.

When I arrived at my next psychiatry appointment I shared the good news with my psychiatrist that my antidepressant was working. I slid into bed at night without the shimmering procession of suicide scenarios rolling through my mind. I passed entire afternoons without feeling that each gust of wind that rustled the leaves of the trees in my backyard was capable of sweeping me into oblivion. My fascination with death hadn't ceased, but it had diminished from infatuation to preoccupation. Despair still descended, but it had loosened into a permeable fog rather than razor sharp edges of hopelessness

Dr. Daly smiled and told me told she was pleased with my progress. She paused before proceeding with her next sentences. We also needed to recognize that my depressive symptoms were still significant, she said. I would benefit strongly from adding a second medication to my regimen.

My guarded look conveyed my doubts. I stiffened my shoulders and waited for her to continue.

Treatment of depression is a complex process, she told me. Her suggested combination of drugs was a known protocol. I would slowly climb the ladder of milligrams. As I ascended I should notice a lightening of the depression and decrease of suicidal thoughts. To limit myself to my current medication would perpetuate high levels of risk for suicidal behavior.

I let the doctor's words hang at the edge of a long silence. I had tasted progress. I wanted to rediscover hope. Her argument was grounded in science. I stared forward, trying to peer into a future shrouded with obscurity, then nodded and told her yes.

Several weeks after starting this second drug I noticed subtle changes in my mood. The rooms in my house were no longer dark caverns for isolating myself from a menacing world. Our nation's spiral into violent civil war wasn't quite as inevitable. Videos of adorable puppies weren't grim reminders of every living creature's struggle to find sustenance and survival in a savage, unforgiving world. I had made the right choice to start this second medication.

These two drugs brought a greater sense of hope but they carried a cost. Irritability made me bristle with constant indignation. When a friend joining us for dinner would slide her chair away from our dining table the abrasive sound of wooden legs scraping across the tile floor made me want to kick this offending piece of furniture out from under her. When my co-worker cleared his throat one too many times in succession I would lean across my desk and growl at him to go buy allergy medicine. I was constantly telling

Daniel to turn down the TV, chew more quietly, wash the dishes better, buy riper bananas, leave for work.

Medication number three was a mood stabilizer. This drug smoothed out the sharp spikes of my emotions. My husband no longer had to gingerly test my temperament before asking me if I wanted cornflakes or Cheerios for breakfast or tell me that my shoelace was untied. I stopped fuming when drivers in front of me allowed elderly pedestrians to inch their way across the crosswalk. Work was no longer a constant struggle to squelch hostile rebuttals to the incompetent people who provided my paycheck.

Months after starting this third medication, I offered praise to my psychiatrist for the cumulative effects of this pharmaceutical trio. They were working in harmony, I told her. I no longer felt that I was only one psychological stumble away from abject despair and incessant suicidal ideation. It wasn't perfection, but it was significant progress.

The doctor told me she had a question for me. How close did I feel I was to the level of well-being that existed before I experienced my major depressive episode?

For a moment I felt like she'd grabbed me by

the shoulders and forcefully shaken me. I don't know if Dr. Daly understood just how profound this question was. I had pondered it almost every day of my life. Articulating the answer was almost impossible.

I took a breath and told her that a return to a pre-depression level of hope was the revered benchmark and Holy Grail that people struggling with major depression dream of. I revealed to her that I grieved for my past life. It was a shimmering mirage that evaporated every time I approached it. I told her that my medications had loosened the crushing grip of depression but the disease was still a constant, hovering presence. It maintained a baleful, watchful position until the moment that it descended.

Dr Daly spoke calmly as she told me there was another medication that might elevate me towards a stronger sense of well-being. It was an adjunct to antidepressants. It was subtle, with few side effects. It could be a potent booster to my existing medications.

Internal alarm bells rang. The uncompromising part of me that had vowed a path of restraint pitched its voice the loudest. I had already betrayed my integrity and become a member of the corrupt society I so firmly rejected. I needed to apply brakes to this reckless journey.

These zealous admonitions clashed with another internal voice stubbornly asserting itself. The possibility, however remote, of returning to a version of the past was deeply compelling. I was no longer appeased by the idea of reducing depression, I was tantalized by the prospect that I might eliminate it. I wanted my former life back, the entire thing. I told the doctor yes.

Two months after starting this fourth medication I was celebrating a friend's birthday at her home. It was a bright Sunday afternoon with an outdoor temperature that seemed to climb even as the evening shadows increased their length over the backyard. A small group of revelers were gathered in the living room, peering over the shoulder of one of our friends as she showed us photos on her phone. These images had been taken only a few minutes earlier, snapped during the moment when the guest of honor blew out the candles on the cake. There were about eight people in the frame. I leaned forward to see this group portrait more clearly, and then frowned as the details came into focus. Something was wrong. A stranger had lodged himself in the midst of the gathering. He was a man with salt and pepper hair, in his mid-fifties, wearing a light blue shirt and holding a glass of red wine in one hand. He had a pudgy, shiny face and a belly that bulged over his belt. A queasy feeling gripped me as I recognized the interloper. The mysterious party guest with the round cheeks and protruding waistline was me.

The next morning I stood in front of the bathroom mirror and stared at the reflection of a man who suddenly seemed to be a stranger. I poked and prodded the flesh of my stomach. Not only was this the bulk of a person who had slid into a state of corpulence, it was the countenance of someone who had slipped into fatigue. My eyes had retreated behind shadowy circles. I was lethargic and listless. I had aged three years in the past two months.

My phone call to my psychiatrist betrayed none of the agitation that I felt. I left a message for her to call me back as soon as possible.

When Dr. Daly returned my call that afternoon I grabbed my phone off my desk at work and hurried to a nearby empty office that offered privacy to those of us who performed our jobs in the sprawling floor of open workstations.

I told Dr. Daly that I needed to stop this medication before my fingers got too fat to be able to enter her phone number. I told her my body resembled a pear that had been genetically enhanced for expanded girth. My main exercise routine consisted of lifting a fork to my mouth in repeat sets throughout the day.

I could imagine her tilting her head in a contemplative pose. Did I feel that my depression had decreased with the addition of this newest drug? she asked.

It's possible, I told her, but the weight gain and fatigue undermined any progress.

Could I regiment my meals more closely? And increase exercise? she asked.

I explained that I drifted off into naps in front of my computer at work, waking with a sudden jerk of my head and reaching for a handful of animal crackers from the box I kept stored in a drawer of my desk.

Dr. Daly had a tone of voice she reserved for our most sensitive interactions. It was a combination of impassive observation mixed with sincerity. I'd heard it before on other unsettling occasions when I'd arrived at junctures of acute uncertainty on how to manage my mental health.

This particular drug takes longer to assimilate but is known to have positive results, she said. She would like for me to try it for two more weeks. Dr. Daly had positioned herself like a sturdy road sign at the crossroads where I balked, pointing towards a preferred direction.

One of depression's most pernicious traits is the power to make its host slink away from conflict. I didn't need the doctor's comments to sabotage my will. I had backed myself into a corner without outside coercion. I told her I would continue the medication.

The following Saturday morning I stood in our kitchen, pondering my schedule for the day. Daniel was in another room, meticulously building a diorama that featured two taxidermied mice dressed in tiny tweed suits, posed in front of their miniature forest cottage. I was on my own for the next several hours.

My plans were modest. I wanted to eat and sleep with periodic interruptions to watch television. I'd already initiated the day's first activity. The cupboard where we kept our supply of snacks was open. The counter in front of me was strewn with several cellophane bags and a jar of peanut butter with a spoon plunged into its center. I pulled a handful of popcorn from a bag and nibbled it. I felt like a surly black bear swiping its meaty paw through a camper's bountiful picnic basket.

In that moment I caught a glimpse of myself from the viewpoint of a judge in a courtroom, seated behind her imposing dais, ready to sentence a repeat offender. The heap of junk food in front of me was the evidence. My burgeoning weight and apathy were the crimes. My sentence would be an extra 25 lbs. and the collapse of self-esteem. I wanted to beg for mercy but my mouth was too full.

I calmly picked up my phone and dialed my psychiatrist's number. I silently rehearsed the words I would leave on Dr. Daly's voice mail. I cleared my throat as the third ring sounded.

The sound of her voice resonating across the digital airwaves sent a shock straight to my vocal cords. The safe haven provided by voicemail had vanished. I managed to say my name and then proceed with a muddled comment about her unexpected presence. She laughed lightly, told me she was catching up on some paperwork on a Saturday morning and informed me I was lucky to catch her.

I launched into a stumbling summary of why this medication was so harmful. The side effects were unbearable. I was overweight and slovenly. I needed to terminate this drug immediately. I ended my speech and let the air rush back into my lungs.

Dr. Daly's voice was a composed counterpart to my own as she told me she appreciated my input. My adverse reaction to this medication was clearly more detrimental than any potential positive results. She concurred that I should stop. She gave me instructions for tapering the dosage over the course of the next month until the drug was eliminated from my body. I told her I agreed with her, and quickly hung up.

I made the first reduction that evening, pressing the edge of the pill cutter blade into the surface of the pill and pressing downward, an executioner delivering the guillotine's edge to the guilty party.

A week later I was able to walk past the cupboards in our kitchen without pivoting out of my path and ravaging the interior. These crunchy, salty, fatty foods had lost their power over me. I resumed my exercise routine, slipping into shorts and running shoes twice a week to jog through the streets of my neighborhood.

As the digital numbers on the bathroom scale gradually declined I felt the sense of accomplishment that comes from dignity regained, but I was also aware of a nucleus of bitterness still smoldering inside me. Surprisingly, it wasn't directed at myself.

There are dozens of medical authorities in our lives. Some of them have advanced medical degrees and some of them are waiters in our local coffee shop. Some of them are close relatives and some are casual acquaintances. Some live in distant cities and some live under our roof. They acquire their expertise from acclaimed universities or from websites that offer crash courses in self-improvement. These concerned companions will share their advice in voices that are graceful or aggressive: we shouldn't stay home so much, it makes us isolated; we shouldn't go out so much, it overwhelms us; we shouldn't work full time, it exhausts us; we should work full time, it engages us; we should increase our medication, it's not working effectively; we should reduce our medication, it's making us confused; we should sleep more, it will rejuvenate us; we shouldn't sleep so much, it makes us lethargic.

Our psychiatrists and psychotherapists are the professionals that help us manage our mental health, but our co-worker with the sky blue eyeshadow may be the one that has personal experience with depression and drops a tidbit of advice that expands our understanding of our disease. We need the waitress as much as we need our psychiatrist, we need our Aunt Yolanda from Duluth as well as our psychotherapist, we need personal and impersonal, objective and subjective, dichotomy and harmony.

One of my most important steps towards managing my depression was the realization that every professed expert—both amateur and educated—is working with limited information. They can become entrenched in their version of our mental health and their vision for our future. We are the only person that has true access to our moods, emotions, feelings, struggles and perceptions. Everyone else relies on speculation and presumption to some degree.

When we suspect that the advice of our friends, colleagues, partners, doctors, relatives and acquaintances is becoming too biased it's time for a change. We need to appoint ourselves as the authority of our own lives. We deserve unconditional support from our allies. We are the kings and queens of our depression. It's time to occupy our throne, survey our kingdom, rattle our jewelry and demand that our court work in our favor. We may have to pitch our voice higher, push harder, rise above our own self-contempt and fear, and assert ourselves. It may take a single effort or a dozen attempts but it is our right and our imperative.

Chapter 15

I stumble into a frustrating question with annoying repetition: why did I develop clinical depression? Is it genetic, is it behavioral, is it environmental, is it random? I don't know. Nobody does. Psychiatry is a form of archaeology, a dig in the dirt to unearth a single artifact or a vast culture. Researchers, scientists and people living with major depressive disorder have their theories and evidence, but none can answer these questions with utter certainty.

I've tried to trace its origins in my life. My relationship with Daniel had become strained in the year leading up to my major depressive episode, but those struggles weren't the first to affect our marriage. Twenty years of shared homes, vacations, beds, sex, meals, germs, friends, flatulence and emotions on a daily basis will test the stamina and stability of even an iron-willed superhero. None of those challenges sent me spiraling into a hospital. Daniel and I grew more adept at communicating each time these threats appeared.

I'd experienced episodes of anxiety throughout my life, but that places me in the ranks of millions of people on every continent who are susceptible to the relentless pulse and pressure of life around them. We all breathe the collective air of worry over money, health, politics, relationships, fear. Yet only a very small percentage of us will go on to experience panic attacks, major depression or suicidal ideation.

I took Flagyl and it created dissociation, which contributed to a precarious sense of reality. But that was a finite period of five days. It may have sparked the depression, but it didn't continue to fuel it.

The fact is, my anxiety attacks have reduced, my relationship with my husband is steady, Flagyl was a one-time prescription. Despite these factors, I still live with major depression. For a long time, I resented the lack of scientific evidence that would explain it. I waited for intervention, or an antidote, or a cure. I no longer wait. A major scientific discovery may revolutionize our treatment of depression tomorrow—and I hope it does—but for today I make my plans based on the knowledge I have.

I used to have a single disaster kit. Now I have two. The first consists of the gray bins that sit on a shelf in my garage. This humble monument to self-reliance is carefully packed with supplies that increase the odds that I will survive a natural disaster.

My second kit prepares me for calamities that arrive not from outside forces but from within the wilderness of my own mind. This kit contains elements both visible and invisible, solid and intangible, local and remote.

The palpable parts are found in my house and in nearby locations. Antidepressant medications occupy a shelf in the bathroom cabinet. My therapist and psychiatrist have their offices within a reasonable drive from my home. 9-1-1 are three buttons I can press anytime on my cell phone.

The intangible part is embedded inside me. Each time I survive a slide into acute despair I expand my ability to manage this disease. The major benefit of surviving a dire mental crisis is the resilience that arises from it. I was unable to avoid the initial mental disaster that brought a dissolution of hope and self-worth, but now I feel increased strength in the face of any future tumult that may come rolling and rumbling without warning.

Printed in Great Britain
by Amazon